ERIC MELVIN is a retired Secondary School Headteacher and a qualified Edinburgh Festival Voluntary Guide taking groups of visitors on walks in Edinburgh's celebrated Old and New Towns. He teaches community education classes, giving talks on aspects of Edinburgh's remarkable history. He is also the author of *A Walk Down Edinburgh's Royal Mile* and *A Walk Through Edinburgh's New Town*, and various Scottish history books for children, including *Mary, Queen of Scots*.

THE GREAT AND THE SMALL ARE THERE

The
Edinburgh of
JOHN KAY

Portraits and tales of everyday life
in Edinburgh's 'Golden Age'

Eric Melvin

For Colvid,

With Very Best Wishes

[signature]

October 2017.

First published in 2017
by Eric Melvin, Edinburgh

ISBN 978 0 9956378 0 1

Designed and typeset by
Mark Blackadder

Printed and bound in Britain by
TJ International, Padstow, Cornwall

Contents

To my dear grand-children
Isla and Rui Melvin

and to their much loved
Granny, Lynda Melvin

Acknowledgements

I would like to express my sincere thanks to Alison Stoddart of the City of Edinburgh Council City Libraries Department for her valued efforts in identifying photographs from the excellent Capital Collections.

I would like to thank Peter Ross of Chiaroscuro Video Production and Digital Arts for the pictures taken from *Kay's Portraits*.

I am very grateful to Craig Statham, National Library of Scotland Maps, Fintan Ryan, National Galleries of Scotland, Dr Helen Scott, City Art Centre, City of Edinburgh Museums, and Dr Emily Goetsch, National Library of Scotland, for their help in providing illustrations.

My thanks to Ian Smith of Scottish Pictures for the Thomas Shepherd prints taken from *Modern Athens*.

I am indebted to Dr Walter Stephen for his careful reading of the text and his helpful suggestions for changes.

Finally I would like to thank Mark Blackadder for his design skills, and Mairi Sutherland for her editorial experience and skills, which have been invaluable in the preparation of this book.

OPPOSITE.
Dr William Laing and his niece: a very rare Kay portrait of a child.

By the la' Harry
This shall not go for Nothing

COCK OF THE GREEN.

J. Kay 1803

CHAPTER 1

Introduction

Writing about the year 1831, the celebrated author Henry Mackenzie noted this comment about one of his fellow-citizens:

> One Kay, who had a little talent for drawing, and published caricatures of persons best known in the town which commonly had a considerable resemblance to the originals, particularly in the air and attitude, which he studies by observing them in the street.

On the north side of Edinburgh's famous High Street, just down from the City Chambers and above the entrance to Foulis Close, a plaque indicates the site of the home of John Kay. Every day, hundreds of folk will pass by and perhaps not notice it, fixed as it is at first floor level above the street. Of those who do, I suspect that very few will have ever heard of John Kay. So who was he and why does he deserve much wider recognition as a chronicler of Edinburgh during its 'Golden Age'? This book will look at the life and times of John Kay whose pencil and engraving skills have left us a unique record of life in the Edinburgh of the second half of the 18th century and the early years of the 19th century.

Edinburgh enjoyed a truly remarkable 18th century. From the despairing years that followed the hugely unpopular 1707 Act of

OPPOSITE.
A typical John Kay portrait: this one is of a golfer named Alexander Mckellar.

1

The plaque to John Kay, Foulis Close on the High Street, Edinburgh.

Union, the burgh emerged from the grim, restricting control of the Church of Scotland to become, by the end of the 18th century, arguably the intellectual capital of western Europe. Physically too the city was transformed. Thanks to the inspired leadership of six-times Lord Provost George Drummond, the city burst from the confines of its medieval walls and embarked on an ambitious plan to build what was called even then the New Town.

John Kay (1742–1826) was a self-taught artist and engraver who had come to Edinburgh as young man to work as a barber and hairdresser. However, in 1785 he abandoned his craft and for nearly forty years he sketched and engraved his contemporaries. Some 329 of his drawings, with accompanying notes, were published posthumously as *Kay's Portraits* in 1837. This remarkable man has left us images of some of the intellectual giants of Edinburgh's 'Golden Age' such as Joseph Black, James Hutton, Sir John Sinclair and Adam Smith; notable eccentrics such as Lords Monboddo and Gardenstone; the formidable Francis McQueen, Lord Braxfield; the notorious Deacon William Brodie and a host of colourful characters who walked past his workshop behind St Giles' Kirk in Edinburgh's Parliament Close.

It had been Kay's intention to publish his 'characters'. To that end he had in 1792 begun the task of drawing up notes to accompany the portraits. He was helped by a rather disreputable character by the name of Callender. Unfortunately the work was not completed during Kay's lifetime. It was left to his friend Hugh Paton to complete the task, although Kay had prepared some brief notes about himself. This is how he summarised his remarkable life:

JOHN KAY, the author of these Prints, was born in April 1742, in a small house a little to the south from Dalkeith, commonly called Gibraltar. His father, Mr John Kay, was a mason in Dalkeith, as well as his two paternal uncles, James and Norman Kay. His mother, Helen Alexander, was heiress to many tenements in Edinburgh and Canongate, out of which she was tricked by the circumvention of some of her own relations. She had still so much confidence in these relations, however, that upon the death of her husband in 1748, she boarded her only son John, then only six years of age, with one of them, who used him extremely ill, and not only neglected but beat and starved him.

While he lived with these savages in Leith, he ran various risks of his life from accidents without doors, as well as from bad usage within; and there is every reason to believe that they really wished his death and took every method to accomplish it except downright murder. On one occasion he was blown into the sea from the ferry-boat stairs, and on another he fell into the water on stepping across the joists below the Wooden Pier, but recovered himself both times, by grasping the steps on one occasion and the joists on the other. But he ran a still greater risk of drowning upon a third occasion, when, happening to be seated on the side of a ship in the harbour, he was accidently pushed overboard, and being taken up for dead, remained in that condition for some time, till one of the sailors, anxious to see him, in his hurry trampled upon his belly, which immediately excited a groan, and produced respiration and articulation. He might have died, however, that same evening, had not other people taken more care of him than his barbarous relations did.

About this time he gave strong proofs of an uncommon genius for drawing, by sketching men, horses, cattle, houses etc., with chalk, charcoal, or pieces of burnt wood, for want of pencils and crayons. But under the government of his cousins, no propensity of this kind was either attended to or encouraged. And, though he himself wished rather to be a mason, the profession of his father and uncles, yet, by some fatality or other, it happened that he was bound apprentice to one George Heriot, a barber in Dalkeith, about the age of thirteen or little more. With this honest man he learned his business, and served six years, during which time, although he did every kind of drudgery work, he was perfectly happy in comparison of the state of tyranny under which he had so long groaned at Leith. When his time was out he came to Edinburgh, where he wrought seven years as a journeyman with different masters, after which he began to think of doing business for himself; but not having the freedom of the city, he was obliged to purchase it from the Society of Surgeon-Barbers, of which corporation he accordingly became a member the 19th December 1771, upon paying about L. 40 sterling [£40, equivalent to about £5,000 today].

This business he carried on with great success for several years, being employed by a number of the principal nobility and gentry in and about Edinburgh. Among other genteel customers, he was employed by the late William Nisbet, Esq. of Dirleton, who not only employed him in town but also took him various jaunts through the country with him in his machine [carriage]; and at last became so fond of him, that for several years before he died, particularly the last two [1782 and 1783], he had him almost constantly with him, by night and by day.

The leisure time he had on these occasions, while he lodged at Mr Nisbet's house [now Archerfield House], afforded him an opportunity, which he took care not to neglect, of gratifying the natural propensity of his genius, by improving himself in drawing; and Mr Nisbet having approved of his exertions, and encouraged him in the pursuit, he executed at this time a great number of miniature paintings – some of which are still in the possession of the family of Dirleton, and the greater part in his own.

A self-portrait of young John Kay painting.

It should have been mentioned earlier in the order of chronology that our hero married, so early as the twentieth year of his age, Miss Lily Steven, who bore him ten children, all of whom died young except his eldest son, William, who was named after Mr Nisbet, and who seems to inherit his father's talent for drawing. Mrs Kay died in March 1785, and after living upwards of two years a widower, our hero married his present wife, Miss Margaret Scott, with whom he now lives very happily.

Mr Nisbet of Dirleton, previous to his death, sensible that, by occupying so much of Mr Kay's time, he could not but hurt his business, although he sent money regularly to Mrs Kay, had often promised to make amends by settling a genteel annuity upon him. This, however, from his debilitated habit of body, was delayed from time to time, till death put it out of his power. But, to the honour of his heir, he was so sensible of Mr Kay's good offices to his father, as well as of his father's intentions, that he voluntarily made a settlement of L.20 [about £2,500 today] per annum for life upon him. After the death of his patron [the Parish Register for Dirleton records the death of William Nisbet of Dirleton Esquire on 1 March 1783 aged 62], our author attempted to etch in aquafortis [nitric acid], and having published some of his Prints executed in this way, he met with so much unexpected success, that he at last determined to drop his

JOHN KAY

Drawn & Engraved by Himself 1786.

old profession altogether, which he did accordingly in 1785.

Our author has drawn himself, in this Print, sitting in a thoughtful posture, in an antiquated chair (whereby he means to represent his love of antiquities) with his favourite cat (the largest it is believed in Scotland) sitting upon the back of it; several pictures hanging behind him; a bust of Homer, with his painting utensils on the table before him, a scroll of paper in his hand, a volume of his works upon his knee.

So Kay suffered a very challenging childhood. But for the kindness of a customer, Mr Nisbet of Dirleton, his natural talent as an artist might never have come to light. He set out for Edinburgh in 1762 with his young wife to further his career as a barber. What would he find? The next two chapters give some background to the city at that time.

CHAPTER 2

The Act of Union and the Porteous Riot

The Edinburgh of the mid 18th century was suffering from an acute lack of confidence. The hugely unpopular Treaty of Union of 1707 had seen the loss not just of Scotland's independence but also the removal of the parliament from the capital.

Popular feeling was very much opposed to the negotiated terms. The Scottish Parliament was flooded with petitions opposing the proposed Union. These came from the burghs, villages, presbyteries and individual groups of people. In all a total of ninety-six petitions were received. Not one petition was received in favour. This petition from the people of Dunfermline was typical of the many that were sent:

> We humbly beseech the Honourable Estates [the Scottish Parliament] and do confidently expect that you will not allow of any such Union; but that you will support and preserve entire the Sovereignty and Independence of this Crown and Kingdom and the Rights and Privileges of Parliament which have been so valiantly maintained by our heroic ancestors for near two thousand years; that the same may be transmitted to succeeding generations as they have been conveyed to us.

In October 1706 Robert Harley, Secretary of State for the Northern Department despatched Daniel Defoe, future author of *Robinson Crusoe,* to Edinburgh to act as an agent for the London government.

A view of early 18th-century Edinburgh from Arthur's Seat.

This is typical of the alarming reports that he sent.

> The rabble attended at the door, and by shouting and noise, having increased their number to several thousands, they began with Sir Patrick Johnson who was one of the Treaters [one of those selected to negotiate the terms of the proposed Treaty of Union], and the year before had been Lord Provost. [Patrick Johnson was Provost in 1700 and 1704 and would serve again in 1708.]
>
> First they assaulted his lodgings with stones and sticks and curses not a few, but his windows being too high, they came up the stairs to his door, and fell to work at it with great hammers, and had they broke it open in their first fury, he had, without doubt, been torn in pieces without mercy; and this only because he was a Treater in the Commission to England for before there was no man so well beloved as he over the whole city.

One by one the Treaty terms were debated and voted on. Many of the debates extended far into the night with contemporary reports

Parliament Close, later Parliament Square, (James Skene, 1829).

of some members literally fainting from exhaustion. The atmosphere at times was electric as speakers clashed violently over the proposed Treaty.

Some of the Treaty terms were passed with very little opposition such as Article 4, which opened up English trade to Scotland. This was passed on a vote of 156 to 19. Others though were fiercely contested with some debates raging far into the night. Feelings were running very high. Outside in the streets of Edinburgh, the mob regularly rioted and broke the windows of those suspected of supporting the proposed Union.

A final attempt was made to force the Scots Parliament to reject the proposed Treaty. A huge demonstration was planned and a formal protest drawn up to be presented to Parliament. The perceived leader of this opposition was the Duke of Hamilton. However, on the day chosen, he took to his bed complaining of toothache. He was prevailed upon to attend later in the day but he prevaricated and the chance was gone. Many opponents of the Treaty lost heart and some withdrew from Parliament in despair. The government pressed on and so finally on 16 January 1707, the Treaty was passed by 110 votes to 67. The Three Estates met for the

last time on 25 March 1707. In drawing proceedings to a close, the
Lord Chancellor, the Earl of Seafield, famously remarked: 'Now
there's ane end of ane auld sang.' Meanwhile, outside, the bells of
St Giles' Kirk tolled the popular tune: 'Why should I feel so sad on
my wedding day?'

While the west of Scotland, and particularly Glasgow, were to
benefit from the opening-up of the English colonies to Scottish
merchants, Edinburgh's traditional trade with Continental Europe
suffered badly throughout the 18th century by the succession of
wars fought between Britain and France. On top of these losses to
prestige and to trade, two further incidents had seriously damaged
Edinburgh's reputation with the government in London. Incredibly
in the space of just ten years, one Lord Provost, Alexander Wilson,
was debarred from office for failing in his duty while another,
Archibald Stewart, was imprisoned in the Tower of London and put
on trial on suspicion of surrendering the city to the Jacobite army
of Bonnie Prince Charlie. Alexander Wilson had the misfortune to
be Lord Provost in 1736 – the year of the notorious Porteous Riots.

An extraordinary series of events in Edinburgh in 1736
prompted the Town Council to issue an Act of Council that was to
be read from the Mercat Cross and at various other points in the
burgh. Part of this Act of Council dated 31 August 1737 reads as
follows:

> The Lord Provost, Baillies and Council . . . taking to their
> consideration that the Peace and good Government of this
> City has been frequently disturbed and insulted, and many
> pernicious and fatal Consequences have ensued to the
> Citizens and Inhabitants thereof, by the most insolent and
> illegal Practice of throwing Stones, Mud and other Garbage,
> at the proper Officers of the Law, City-guard and Common
> Executioner, when in the Exercise of their Duty and Office
> at lawful and public Executions of Criminals . . . That the
> Person or Persons who shall be hereafter found guilty . . .
> shall, upon their being convicted thereof, be whipt through
> the City by the hand of the Common Hangman, and there-
> after be imprisoned for the Space of one Year . . .

The practice of throwing 'Stones, Mud, Dung, or other Garbage at the Officers of the Law' at public executions was a long-standing Edinburgh tradition. Something though had gone seriously wrong to prompt this draconian reaction from the Edinburgh authorities.

There was a long history of serious rioting in the burgh. In 1679 the first Town Guard of twenty 'Greycoats' was recruited. However, they proved to be totally ineffective in dealing with the frequent street riots, particularly an apprentice riot of 1682 and a further riot of 1686 described by Hugo Arnot in his *History of Edinburgh* published in 1779.

> The public attendance upon Mass by the chief officers of state about this time excited a tumult in Edinburgh. A rabble of apprentices and others, insulted the Chancellor's lady and other persons of distinction when returning from their chapel. The affront was resented by great severity. A journeyman baker being ordered by the Privy Council to be whipped through the Canongate for being concerned in the riot, the mob rose, rescued him from punishment, beat the executioner and continued all night in uproar. The King's foot guards and soldiers from the Castle were brought to assist the Town Guard in quelling this disturbance. They fired among the mob and killed two men and a woman. Next day several were scourged; but the Privy Council were so afraid of the populace that they appointed a double file of musketeers and pikemen to prevent the sufferers [those being publicly whipped through the streets] being rescued.

The Edinburgh legend suggests that the shot woman was pregnant and that the baby was successfully cut from its dying mother's body.

The new Town Guard was formed on 1 June 1689. This comprised a company of between 120 and 200 men, mostly recruited from veterans of the British Army. Many of them had served in Highland regiments. The men wore redcoats like regular soldiers and were armed with muskets, pikes and the fearsome Lochaber axes. They were commanded by a Captain, again usually a former regular British Army officer, appointed by the Town Council. The Guardsmen were described in his *Memorials* by Lord Cockburn thus: 'They were all old, hard-featured, red-nosed veterans much given to whisky and the insults of small boys.'

The famous Edinburgh poet Robert Fergusson, whom Robert Burns was to acknowledge as 'my father in the Muse', and who was to die tragically in the Edinburgh Asylum in 1774 at the young age of twenty-four, wrote of the Town Guard in 'The Daft Days', his first published poem:

> And thou, great God o' aqua vitae   [alcoholic drink]
> Wha swayst the empire o' this city;
> When fou we're sometime capernoity,   [behaving riotously]
> Be thou prepared.
> To save us frae that black banditti   [thugs]
> The City Guard!

Fergusson had another dig at the Town Guard in his poem 'Hallow Fair':

> Gud folk, as ye come frae the fair
> Bide yont frae this Black squad;
> There's nae sic savages elsewhere
> Allowed to wear cockade

Given his riotous lifestyle and his love of the bottle, Fergusson no doubt had fallen foul of the Town Guard (see Plate 3).

For many years most public executions were carried out in the Grassmarket. Edward Topham, an English visitor to Edinburgh, described one such execution that he witnessed on 9 December 1774.

> The town of Edinburgh from the amazing height of its buildings, seems particularly formed to make a spectacle of this kind, solemn and affecting. The houses from the bottom up to the top, were lined with people, every window crowded with spectators to see the unfortunate man [John Reid, convicted of sheep-stealing, who had been defended by James Boswell, the diarist and biographer of Dr Johnson], pass by. At one o' clock the City Guard went to the Tolbooth, the common gaol here, to receive and conduct their prisoner to the place of execution which is always in the Grass Market … All the remaining length of the High Street was filled with

SHON DOW

KAY. *fecit* 1784

Town Guardsman John Dhu, drawn by John Kay. The Highlander once killed an Edinburgh rioter with a blow from his Lochaber axe.

people, many from the country around, whom the novelty of the sight had brought together . . .

On the Guard knocking on the door of the Tolbooth, the unhappy criminal made his appearance. He was dressed in a white waistcoat and breeches, usual on these occasions, bound with black ribands, with a white nightcap tied with the same . . . Two clergymen accompanied him and were discoursing with him on subjects of religion . . .

The Executioner, who seemed ashamed of the meanness of his office, followed muffled up in a great coat, and the City Guards, with their arms ready, marched around him. The criminal, whose hands were tied behind him and the rope about his neck, walked up the remaining part of the street. When the criminal had descended three parts of the hill which leads to the Grassmarket, he beheld the crowd waiting for his coming and the instrument of execution waiting at

the end of it. He made a short stop here, naturally shocked at such a sight, and the people seemed to sympathise with his affliction. When he reached the end he recalled his resolution; and after passing some time in prayer with the clergymen and once addressing himself to the people, he was turned off and expired.

Perhaps John Kay was amongst the thousands of spectators who witnessed John Reid's execution.

In 1736 the Town Guard was commanded by Captain John Porteous, a veteran of the French wars. He was a man with a bad temper and an over-fondness of the bottle. One contemporary, Alexander Carlyle, later commented that: 'This man by his skill in many exercise, particularly the golf, and by his gentlemanly behaviour, was admitted in to the company of his superiors, which elated his mind, and added insolence to his native roughness so that he was much hated and feared by the mob of Edinburgh.'

Despite his reputation for coarseness, Porteous had been among the first subscribers to pay for the building of the planned Edinburgh Royal Infirmary. Sir Walter Scott, who used the Porteous Riots as the basis for his famous novel *The Heart of Midlothian* published in 1818, has left us this description of Captain Porteous based on the memories of those who knew him:

> He was about middle size, short and well-made having a military air, and yet rather a gentle and mild countenance. His complexion was brown; his face somewhat fretted with the scars of the smallpox; his eyes rather languid than keen or fierce. On the present occasion however, it seemed to those who saw him as if he were agitated by some evil demon. His step was irregular; his voice hollow and broken; his countenance pale; his eyes staring and wild; his speech imperfect and confused, and his whole appearance so disordered, that many remarked that he seemed to be fey, a Scottish expression meaning the state of those who are driven to their impending fate by the strong impulse of some irresistible necessity.

OPPOSITE. Preparing for an execution in the Grassmarket (James Skene, 1827).

The 15th-century Old Tolbooth: the prison and a site of public execution, demolished in 1817.

Early in 1736, Andrew Wilson, a well-known smuggler, had been surprised by excise men and lost his smuggled goods. Along with young George Robertson and two others, he broke into the excise house in Anstruther to recover the smuggled goods but was captured with his gang. All were brought to Edinburgh for trial. The two others were sentenced to transportation but Wilson and Robertson were sentenced to death. A Malt Tax had been introduced in 1725 which increased the price of drink so smugglers bringing in wine and brandy from the Continent attracted a lot of popular sympathy. A file was smuggled to the two men in the Tolbooth. The bars of their cell window were removed. Wilson, who was a bulky man, went first but got stuck. The noise alerted the guards and so the escape bid failed. Wilson was dismayed that he had not let the younger man go first.

As was customary the two condemned men were taken to St Giles' Kirk for the morning service on the Sunday before their execution. What happened next was witnessed by the fourteen-year-old Alexander Carlyle, in later life to become minister of Inveresk parish and Moderator of the General Assembly of the Church of Scotland.

OPPOSITE. James Burnet, the last captain of the Edinburgh Town Guard.

I. KAY. 1814.

In those days it was usual to bring the criminals who were condemned to death into the church to attend public worship every Sunday after their condemnation, when the clergyman made some part of his discourse and prayers to suit their situation; which among other circumstances of solemnity which then attended the state of condemned criminals, had no small effect upon the public mind. Robertson and Wilson were smugglers, and had been condemned for robbing a custom-house, where some of their goods had been deposited; a crime which at that time did not seem, in the opinion of the common people, to deserve so severe a punishment. I was carried [taken] by an acquaintance to church to see the prisoners on the Sunday before the execution. We went early into the church on purpose to see them come in, and were seated in a pew before the gallery in front of the pulpit. Soon after we went into the church by the door from the Parliament Close, the criminals were brought in by the door next the Tolbooth, and placed in a long pew, not too far from the pulpit. Four soldiers [Town Guardsmen] came in with them, and placed Robertson at the head of the pew, and Wilson below him, two of themselves sitting below Wilson, and two in a pew behind him.

The bells were ringing and the doors were open, while the people were coming into the church. Robertson watched his opportunity, and, suddenly springing up, got over the pew into the passage that led in to the door in the Parliament Close, and no person offering to lay hands on him, made his escape in a moment – so much the more easily, perhaps, as everybody's attention was drawn to Wilson, who was a stronger man, and who, attempting to follow Robertson, was seized by the soldiers, and struggled so long with them that the two who at last followed Robertson were too late. It was reported that he [Wilson] had maintained his struggle that he might let his companion have time.

The magistrates were very angry with Captain Porteous, who was in bed with a hangover. An enraged Porteous ordered Wilson to be kept in chains. This barbarous act was bitterly resented. The execution was set for 14 April 1736. The town was packed with onlookers. Fearing an attempt at rescue, a detachment of soldiers from Edinburgh Castle was brought in to line the streets. Porteous took this as a personal insult.

Again we have the eyewitness account of young Alexander Carlyle who was taken up to a tenement window by one of his university tutors, Patrick Baillie, to watch the execution. Carlyle was dreading the occasion as he had recently witnessed an execution in Dumfries at which the prisoner, Jock Johnstone, had attempted to break free on the scaffold and had had to be violently restrained.

Mr Baillie had taken windows in a house on the north side of the Grassmarket, for his pupils and me, in the second floor, about seventy or eighty yards westward of the place of execution, where we went in due time to see the show . . . When we arrived at the house, some people who were looking from the windows were displaced, and went to a window in the common stair about two feet below the level of ours. The street is long and wide and there was a very great crowd assembled. The execution went on with the usual forms, and Wilson behaved in a manner very becoming his situation. There was not the least appearance of an attempt to rescue; but soon after the executioner had done his duty, there was an attack made upon him, as usual on such occasions, by the boys and blackguards throwing stones and dirt in testimony of their abhorrence of the hangman. But there was no attempt to break through the guard and cut down the prisoner.

It was generally said that there was very little, if any, more violence than had usually happened on such occasions. Porteous, however, inflamed with wine and jealousy, thought proper to order his Guard to fire, their muskets being loaded with slugs; and when the soldiers showed reluctance, I saw him turn to them with threatening gesture and inflamed countenance. They obeyed, and fired; but wishing to do as little harm as possible, many of them elevated their pieces, the effect of which was that some people were wounded in the windows; and one unfortunate lad [Henry Graham, a young tailor from the Canongate] whom we had displaced was killed in the stair window by a slug entering his head . . .

We had seen many people, women and men, fall on the street, and at first thought that it was only through fear, and by their crowding on one another to escape. But when the crowd dispersed, we saw them lying dead or wounded, and had no longer any doubt of what had happened. The numbers were said to be eight or nine killed, and double the number wounded; but this was never exactly known.

Another eyewitness, the poet Allan Ramsay, confirms much of Carlyle's account:

After he [Wilson] was cut down and the guard drawing up to go off, some unlucky boys threw a stone or two at the hangman, which is very common, on which the brutal Porteous (who it seems had ordered his party to load their guns with ball) let drive first himself amongst the innocent mob and commanded his men to follow his example which quickly cleansed the street but left three men, a boy and a woman dead upon the spot, besides several others wounded, some of whom are dead since. After this first fire he took it in his head when half up the Bow to order another volley & kill'd a tailor in a window three stories high, a young gentleman & a son of Mr Matheson the minister's and several more were dangerously wounded and all this from no more provocation than what I told you before, the throwing of a stone or two that hurt no body. Believe this to be true, for I was an eye witness and within a yard or two of being shot as I sat with some gentlemen in a stabler's window opposite to the Gallows. After this the crazy brute march'd with his ragamuffins to the Guard [the Tolbooth], as if he had done nothing worth noticing but was not long there till the hue and cry rose from them that had lost friends & servants, demanding justice . . . I could have acted more discreetly had I been in Porteous's place.

The Guard retreated to the Tolbooth followed by a raging mob. The magistrates arrested Porteous and charged him with murder. He was put on trial on 5 July and condemned to death. He was now locked in the same cell in the Tolbooth, recently occupied by Wilson and

Robertson. In desperation Porteous appealed to Queen Caroline in London, who was acting as Regent while her husband, George II, was in Flanders with the army. Porteous disputed the evidence that had been led against him and concluded with a claim that, faced with the fury of the mob, he and his men had to defend themselves:

> But in case your Petitioner [Porteous] had been guilty either of firing, or ordering his Men to fire, upon the Occasion aforesaid, your Petitioner most humbly intreats your Majesty to consider, that your Petitioner was in the Exercise of a Trust delegated to him by the lawful Civil Authority; that he and his Detachment were first unlawfully assaulted and invaded by the Populace, and that divers [several] of his Men bruised and hurt; and if, in the Case of such an Insult upon the Laws, your Petitioner had proceeded to repel Force by Force, your Petitioner humbly begs leave to observe, that tho' he shou'd look back with the utmost Sorrow upon so fatal an Event, yet he humbly hopes, that the Provocation and Aggression aforesaid, wou'd be considered by your most excellent Majesty, in your profound Wisdom as a great extenuation of an Offence, which could not be supposed to be attended with any prepense [sic – intentional] Malice of your Petitioner, against Persons of whom he had no knowledge; and that your Petitioner would be deemed a proper object of the Royal Clemency.
>
> (Petition of Captain John Porteous to her Majesty, Queen Caroline, July 1736)

On the advice of Robert Walpole, Queen Caroline granted a suspension of the sentence of death for six weeks. This was seen by many in Edinburgh as a reprieve. It also re-awoke a smouldering resentment of what was seen as interference by England in Scotland's affairs. It touched the raw nerve of anti-Union sentiment that still ached.

The events of the night of 7 September have been well described by Sir Walter Scott in his famous novel *The Heart of Midlothian* published in 1818 – the seventh in the series of what became known as the Waverley Novels. The gates of the burgh were seized; a crowd of several thousand, many masked or in disguise, marched on the Tolbooth:

The cloaths [sic] which appeared under their different
disguises, as well as the conduct and deliberation with which
their plan was executed, bespoke many among them to be
superior to the vulgar; and the violence they committed
proceeded not from the rash and unpremeditated concert
of a rabble. They surprised and disarmed the town–guard,
[and] blocked up the gates of the city, to prevent the
admission of troops quartered in the suburbs. The prison-
doors, which would not yield to the force of their hammers,
they consumed by fire. The prisoners they dismissed,
(Porteous excepted), whom they threatened with the tragical
catastrophe which he dreaded. In vain did the magistrates
endeavour to quell or appease the ferment. They were pelted
with stones, and threatened to be fired upon. The member
of Parliament for the city went to General Moyle,
commander of the forces in Scotland, and intreated [sic] his
immediate assistance, by the introduction of troops into the
town; but this the General refused, because he had no
written order from the magistrates to that effect; which
indeed, Mr Lindsay, the member [of Parliament], in such
confusion could neither obtain, nor venture to carry about
his person through the midst of an enraged populace.

(Hugo Arnot, *The History of Edinburgh*, 1779, pp. 207–8)

The mob hauled the terrified Porteous down from the chimney that
he had hidden in. Still in his nightclothes he was lashed to a chair,
his red captain's jacket thrown over his shoulders and then carried
down to the Grassmarket. A shop in the West Bow was broken into.
A rope was taken and a guinea left on the counter to pay for it. 'After
reproaching him with his barbarity, they hanged him on the post,
and dispersed quietly, without committing any other outrage or
disturbance whatever.'

The government in London was outraged. Alexander Wilson,
the Lord Provost was summoned to appear before a Cabinet
committee and was locked in the Tower for three months. The
Town Walls were to be demolished and the Town Guard disbanded.
However, these threats were later dropped. A huge reward was
offered for information leading to the conviction of those responsible but to no avail. Apart from two servants who were put on trial

The Porteous Riot by James Skene, 1823.

but acquitted, no-one was ever identified as being involved and yet thousands knew but no-one ever told.

Writing not long after the event, the Edinburgh lawyer and historian Hugo Arnot commented:

> It is very remarkable that although forty years have now elapsed, no information has been offered, no discovery made of those concerned in this conspiracy. Notwithstanding the high rewards offered to informers, and the number of people whom it behoved to be engaged in it; but a fidelity has shown which none but people acting from principle could have observed.

The site of the Tolbooth – 'The Heart of Midlothian' in the pavement near St Giles' Kirk in the High Street.

'All passion spent': A modern stone in Greyfriars Kirkyard marks the spot of Captain Porteous's grave.

And as for Porteous, he was buried in nearby Greyfriars Kirkyard with a simple stone marked 'P' and the date 1736. In 1973 a new headstone was erected recording his murder and finishing with the words 'All passion spent.'

CHAPTER 3

Edinburgh
and the '45

In 1747, the Edinburgh bookseller Gideon Crawford published a book with a sensational title – *The Trial of Archibald Stewart for neglect of Duty, and Misbehaviour in the execution of his Duty as Lord Provost of Edinburgh*. The charge related to the perceived failure of the Lord Provost to properly defend Edinburgh from the advancing Jacobite army of The Young Pretender – Bonnie Prince Charlie. Indeed there were those who accused the Lord Provost of deliberately allowing the city to fall into Jacobite hands and that he should have been tried for treason.

Perhaps a very early memory for John Kay was the sight of armed Highland clansmen foraging for food around his home outside Dalkeith. On 17 September 1745, Edinburgh had been captured, without a shot being fired in its defence, by the Jacobite army of Charles Edward Stuart – known to history as 'the Young Pretender' or 'Bonnie Prince Charlie' (see Plate 4). It was not just the Scottish capital that had been taken by surprise, the whole country was astonished that in just over four weeks, Charles had captured Edinburgh, defeated the only Government army in Scotland and was poised to invade England in an attempt to regain the throne for his father, the exiled James Stuart. Charles had landed on the remote Outer Hebridean island of Eriskay on 23 July 1745. However, he had landed with just a handful of supporters. His supply ship, with men, weapons and money, had been intercepted by the Royal Navy and forced back to France. Undaunted, Charles sailed to the Scottish mainland and on 19 August had raised his standard at Glenfinnan.

News of the Jacobite threat was first received in Edinburgh on 8
August. The Lord Provost Archibald Stewart received a letter from
the Marquis of Tweeddale warning him that Charles had sailed
from France. Shortly after, Lord President Duncan Forbes of
Culloden reported that Charles had landed and that 'Moidart was
all aflame.' It is hard to imagine the shock with which this news
must have been received. Was Charles marching southwards? Was
he accompanied by a large French army? Had all the Highland clans
risen in support of the young prince? There was such a lack of hard
information. At first the government of George II in London
refused to take the news seriously. But then as the reports of Charles'
landing were confirmed, the Commander-in-Chief of the British
Army was recalled from the Continent. This was the twenty-four
year-old Duke of Cumberland, a younger son of George II and a
cousin of Charles. However, the British Army was not in good shape
having been recently beaten by a French army at the Battle of
Fontenoy on 11 May.

There had of course been previous attempts by the Jacobites to
win back the throne. The 1715 Rebellion had stalled at the Battle of
Sherrifmuir near Stirling. There had been a bold plot to capture
Edinburgh Castle but this had been thwarted. The Rebellion of 1719
had been defeated at the Battle of Glen Shiel, when a combined
Jacobite and Spanish force had been scattered. Now some twenty-
six years later, news that there was a fresh invasion must have been
frightening. Duncan Forbes of Culloden met with Lieutenant-
General John Cope, the senior officer in Scotland, to discover to his
dismay that Cope had only 2,000 men at his command. The bulk
of the British Army was in the Low Countries fighting the French.
Cope determined to move northwards to Stirling and from there
to Fort Augustus to prevent Charles reaching the Lowlands. Two
Dragoon regiments were to remain – Gardiner's to cover the Forth
crossings and Hamilton's to guard the port of Leith. Edinburgh
Castle was to be re-provisioned and reinforced by two companies
of Lascelles' Regiment. Forbes meantime made his way north to his
home at Culloden House near Inverness, hoping to persuade the
neighbouring clan chiefs to remain loyal to the House of Hanover.
On 19 August Cope marched his guns and 2,000 troops northwards
to confront Prince Charles.

However, the Jacobites out-marched Cope using the new

military roads laid down by General Wade. Cope headed for Aberdeen and sent an urgent message to Edinburgh for transports south. Those vessels only sailed on 10 September. On 14 September, the burgh was shocked to learn that the Prince, having captured Perth, had crossed the Forth unopposed. That day all the cash held by the Bank of Scotland and the Royal Bank was carried to the Castle. The defence of Edinburgh rested with Lord Provost Archibald Stewart and the small garrison of the Castle commanded by 86-year-old General Guest.

On 27 August, Stewart had convened a meeting of leading citizens in St Giles' Kirk. It was quickly established that all that was available to defend the burgh were the Train Bands of 1,200 men, not mustered since 1688, the 120 men of the Town Guard and the two regiments of dragoons (Hamilton's and Gardiner's). It was agreed to form a regiment of volunteers but the senior judges present, including the Lord Advocate Lord Craigie, pointed out that this required Royal approval. So a rider had to be sent post-haste to London to obtain the necessary permission. This was only obtained on 9 September. A corps of 418 volunteers was recruited

St Giles' Kirk (James Skene, 1817).

including the young Alexander Carlyle (our eye-witness for the Porteous Riots) and William Robertson, future Principal of Edinburgh University. The Commander of these Volunteers was former Lord Provost, George Drummond. These Volunteers were issued with weapons and ammunition from the Castle and drilled in the grounds of the University.

Meanwhile the University's Professor of Mathematics, Colin McLaurin, took charge of preparing the town's defences, including the hurried repairs of the ancient Flodden Wall. There were those though who thought that Lord Provost Stewart was less than enthusiastic about defending the burgh. Some even questioned his loyalty.

According to Alexander Carlyle, who was present as a Volunteer:

> There was not a Whig in the town who did not suspect that [Stewart] favoured the Pretender's cause; and however cautiously he acted in his capacity as chief magistrate, there were not a few who suspected that his backwardness and coldness in the measure of arming the people, was part of a plan to admit the Pretender into the city . . . if that part of the town council who were Whigs had found good ground to have put Stewart under arrest, the city would have held out.

On Saturday 14 September, a group of horsemen galloped into the High Street to report that Charles had crossed the Forth evading Gardiner's men and was now at Linlithgow – just 20 miles (32 km) from Edinburgh. The town was in a panic. Many seized what belongings they could and fled Edinburgh. Others hastily buried their valuables, fearful of the reputation of the advancing Highlanders.

On Sunday 15 September news arrived that Charles was at Linlithgow and advancing on Edinburgh. There was widespread panic. The Town Bell in the Tolbooth was rung for another public meeting in St Giles. What to do? The city was in turmoil. Many citizens fled seeking safety in the surrounding countryside. It must have been a very anxious night. Next morning the town was awoken by the ringing of the bell of the Tolbooth. This was the signal for

OPPOSITE. Alexander Carlyle, drawn by John Kay.

The preserver of the Church from Fanaticism

the Volunteers to assemble in the High Street. They were led off by the two regiments of Dragoons who had been ordered to join Gardiner's Regiment which was stationed to the west of the burgh at Corstorphine. Observers noted that many of the Dragoons looked terrified.

Led by former Lord Provost George Drummond – a man who had fought against the Jacobites at the 1715 Battle of Sherrifmuir – the Volunteers marched down the West Bow amid scenes of great emotion. By the time that they reached the Grassmarket, one-third had deserted. The remainder halted and were refreshed with bread, cheese and ale from the local taverns. Meanwhile the University contingent of staff and students was prevailed upon by the principal, Dr Wishart, to abandon the march. The remaining Volunteers were marched back to the College Yards where they were dismissed by Drummond.

A group of them met in Mrs Turnbull's tavern by the Tron and agreed to hand in their muskets. Some headed for Dunbar to meet up with the expected arrival of General Cope. Others took their places on the Town Wall as night fell. At 1.00am a very pale-looking Provost Stewart visited the Volunteer guards staring fearfully into the darkness. One of the guards caused panic by firing his musket thinking that the Highlanders were approaching. It was only in daylight that it was seen that he had shot a cow.

Next morning the citizens were alarmed to hear the distant sound of musket fire from west of the burgh. Had the Dragoons and the Town Guard managed to fight off the Jacobites? They soon got their answer as from the heights of the Old Town, they saw the red-coated Dragoons come trotting along the country lane known as The Lang Dykes which ran just to the north of present-day Princes Street. The Dragoons halted, gave a cheer and then galloped off eastwards away from the burgh. They were abandoning Edinburgh to its fate. They were followed by a straggling line of women and baggage which sought refuge in the Castle. It was later established that, at Coltbridge by the Water of Leith, the Dragoons had fired one volley at the sight of the approaching Highlanders and then fled leaving the Town Guard to surrender. This became known as 'The Coltbridge Canter'. Ironically as the Dragoons were fleeing, the ships carrying the army of General Cope were sighted in the Firth of Forth. Being warned off from landing at Leith,

Edinburgh's port, they sailed further eastwards towards Dunbar. There they disembarked.

The Town Bell was rung again for a public meeting in the Goldsmiths' Hall which overflowed into St Giles' Kirk. Should the burgh fight to defend itself or surrender hoping that the citizens would be spared from violence? Provost Stewart was trying to maintain some sort of order when the doors of St Giles swung open and a Jacobite officer strode in. He handed a letter to Provost Stewart demanding the burgh's surrender.

From our Camp [Gray's Mill] 16 September 1745

Being now in a condition to make our way into the capital of his Majesty's ancient kingdom of Scotland, he hereby summons you to receive us, as you are in duty bound to do; and in order to it, we hereby require you, on receipt of this, to summon the Town-council, and to take proper measures for securing the peace of the city, which we are desirous to protect. But if you suffer any of the usurper's [George II] troops to enter the town, or any of the cannon, arms, or ammunition now in it, whether belonging to the public or to private persons to be carried off, we shall take it as a breach of your duty, and a heinous offence against the king and us, and shall resent it accordingly. We promise to preserve all the rights and liberties of the city, and the particular property of every one of his majesty's subjects. But if any opposition be made to us, we cannot answer for the consequences, being firmly resolved, at any rate, to enter the city; and in that case, if any of the inhabitants are found in arms against us, they must not expect to be treated as prisoners of war.

CHARLES, P.R.

It was agreed to send a deputation to meet with Charles now close to Edinburgh at Gray's Mill and to hand in the remaining weapons held by the Volunteers. But curiously the 1,000 muskets held by the Town Guard were not surrendered and were later seized by the occupying Highlanders. Was this treachery? This incident was certainly used as evidence in the subsequent trial of Provost Stewart.

That evening a deputation led by former Lord Provost John

Coutts set out to meet with Charles at Gray's Mill. Meanwhile as darkness fell, Cameron of Lochiel, chief of the Clan Cameron, and Sir John Murray of Broughton, an Edinburgh man who had been appointed as Secretary to Charles, led a party of Cameron High-landers to try to gain entry through the Netherbow Port. The gate was opened when the coach that had taken the deputation to Gray's Mill returned. The Jacobites seized their chance and slipped in. The terrified guards fled. Edinburgh had been captured without any resistance being offered. In the morning, Edinburgh folk woke up to find the Camerons drawn up in Parliament Square.

The *Caledonian Mercury* for 18 September captured the aston-ishment of the citizens at this remarkable sequence of events:

> Affairs in this city and neighbourhood have taken the most surprising turn since yesterday, without the least bloodshed or opposition, so that we now have in our streets High-landers and bagpipes in place of Dragoons and drums.

Charles entered Edinburgh by way of Grange Loan, to the south of the burgh, keeping his men out of range of the Castle's guns. He stopped for refreshment at Grange House where legend has it he was presented with a white rose – the famous white cockade – by Lady Ann Seton, sister-in-law of Sir Andrew Lauder, the owner of the house. From there his army made its way eastwards along the line of the present West and East Mayfield Roads to enter Holyrood Park. Crowds turned out to see him. He was wearing a tartan outfit with a blue sash, red velvet breeches, a green velvet bonnet and his white cockade. Charles was cheered into Holyrood Palace where he set up his headquarters.

Meanwhile in Edinburgh at 1.00pm a Proclamation was read out from the Mercat Cross by five very reluctant Royal Heralds and a trumpeter. The Lord Lyon King of Arms, Alexander Brodie, had fled. 'Our dearest son Charles, Prince of Wales, to be sole Regent of our kingdoms of England, Scotland and Ireland with our Dominions...'

The bells of St Giles were rung. Now for General Cope.

The Battle of Prestonpans was fought early in the morning of 21 September. Guided by a local man, the Jacobites crept down through marshy ground and took up position to the east of General

The Netherbow Port, the main entrance to the medieval city of Edinburgh
(James Skene, 1817).

Cope's encampment. As dawn broke, the Jacobite Highlanders
charged. The terrified redcoats broke and ran. Six hundred Government soldiers were killed, including Colonel Gardiner, commander
of the Dragoons. Many more were captured. The Jacobites lost only

thirty-six, all killed. General Cope fled on horseback to Berwick. Charles was now in almost total control of Scotland.

Several fugitives from the battle sought refuge in the Castle. These included a troop of Light Dragoons who had been pursued single-handedly by Colquhoun Grant of Burnside. He chased them to the gates of the Castle and then made his way on horseback down the High Street watched by an awe-struck crowd of onlookers. He stopped at a shop in the Luckenbooths to order himself a new tartan outfit and then made his way down through the Netherbow Port towards the Palace with his bloodstained sword in his hand and his clothes also bloodstained. After Culloden, he had to remain in hiding on his father's estates for many months. Eventually he was able to return to Edinburgh where he practised as a lawyer. He lived long enough to be drawn by John Kay in 1789. Colqhoun Grant died in 1792.

Charles now turned his attention to capturing Edinburgh Castle. However, the Jacobites lacked any heavy artillery so there was little chance of storming the fortress. Instead Charles determined to starve the garrison into surrender. The command of the Castle had now passed from General Guest to the 86-year-old General Preston, a determined Scot who had no intention of surrendering to Charles. If Charles would not lift the siege, then the burgh would be fired on by the Castle's guns.

The bombardment of Edinburgh began on 4 October together with volleys fired by the defendants from a trench dug on the Castlehill. The damage caused was considerable. Several citizens were killed; many more were wounded. Hundreds of terrified townsfolk fled from the town and headed for Leith only to be met by hundreds of people fleeing from Leith as two Royal Navy warships – HMS *Fox* and HMS *Ludlow Castle* – opened fire. There was general rejoicing when news reached Edinburgh two weeks later that HMS *Fox* had hit rocks off Dunbar and had sunk with all hands. The bombardment of the City continued the next day forcing Charles to call off the blockade.

Charles had hoped that his army would be joined by recruits from Edinburgh and the surrounding Lowlands. He was to be

OPPOSITE. Kay drew several characters who had fought against each other in the '45. Colquhoun Grant is the figure on the right.

Above and opposite. Cannonball House at the foot of the Castle Esplanade has two cannonballs lodged in its walls, reputedly souvenirs of the 1745 siege. They can be seen above the lower windows.

sorely disappointed. While many Edinburgh ladies showed their support for Charles, their menfolk went into hiding. Few joined the Jacobite army. Instead many Highlanders now began to desert and left for their homes. Charles wasted precious time entertaining at Holyrood and charming the Edinburgh ladies.

On 22 October a final council meeting was held by Charles at Holyrood Palace. He left Holyrood on 31 October for Pinkie House just outside Edinburgh where he reviewed 5,500 men drawn up by

Lord George Murray. The Jacobites then marched southwards reaching Derby on 7 December. They were only some 120 km from a panic-stricken London. However, the British Army was streaming back from the Continent. Field Marshal Wade, brought out of retirement, threatened to cut the Jacobites off from Scotland. With his Highland commanders arguing against a further advance, Charles reluctantly agreed to retreat back to Scotland. That long retreat ended in total defeat at the battle of Culloden fought outside Inverness on 16 April 1746. Charles was now a fugitive with a price on his head. After many adventures, Charles escaped back to France in September. The Jacobite dream was over.

News of Culloden reached Edinburgh on 19 April. The victorious Duke of Cumberland paraded through the town. The fourteen Jacobite standards captured at Culloden were burnt at the Mercat Cross. Lord Provost Archibald Stewart was arrested and tried for neglect of his duty on 24 March 1747 but acquitted. He was replaced as Lord Provost by George Drummond.

CHAPTER 4

The Challenge
to the Kirk

About the year 1762, the 20-year-old John Kay arrived in Edinburgh
with his young wife, Lily Stevens, whom he had recently married.
He was looking for work and a place for them both to stay. Kay
had completed his apprenticeship as a barber and wigmaker
working for George Heriot in Dalkeith. Now he needed employment as a trained journeyman hoping to build up a customer base
and enough money to apply for membership of the Society of
Surgeon-Barbers of Edinburgh. Scotland's capital though was in a
rather depressed state and was sadly lacking in confidence.
Edinburgh was no longer the seat of government. Since 1707, many
enterprising Scots now saw their futures in London or the
expanding British colonies.

Given the challenges of the Porteous Riot and the occupation
by the Jacobites, Edinburgh was very much under a cloud. To make
matters worse, the burgh's traditional trade across the North Sea
to Continental Europe and Scandinavia was being seriously
disrupted by the French Wars of the Hanoverian Government.
Scotland too was under something of a cloud as far as the government in London was concerned and was often referred to
contemptuously as 'North Britain'.

There was much economic hardship – a fact reported on by
Daniel Defoe who compared Edinburgh's ailing economy with
that of Glasgow which was now benefiting from the Act of Union
which had opened up the former English colonies to Scottish
merchants.

> Glasgow is a city of business; here is the face of trade, as well
> foreign as home trade; and I may say, 'tis the only city in
> Scotland, at this time, that apparently increases and improves
> in both. The Union has answered its end to them more than
> to any other part of Scotland, for this trade is new-formed by
> it; and, as the Union opened the door to the Scots in our
> American colonies, the Glasgow merchants presently fell in
> with the opportunity; and though, when the Union was
> making, the rabble of Glasgow made the most formidable
> attempt to prevent it, yet, now they know better, for they have
> the greatest addition to their trade by it imaginable.

So the first few years of married life for Kay and his growing family
must have been very hard. He and his wife also had to cope with
the loss of children. Lily was to bear him ten children over their
twenty-three years of marriage but only one survived into
adulthood and even he died young.

To add to Edinburgh's depressed state of affairs was the control
of the Church of Scotland over the country's educational, social and
cultural life. The 1688 'Glorious Revolution' had seen the Catholic
James VII of Scotland and II of England forced from the throne to
be replaced by his daughter Mary and her husband the Protestant
William of Orange. One consequence had been the re-establish-
ment of the Church of Scotland's control of the religious life of the
country. And this was a very fundamentalist Church of Scotland
which drew its inspiration from the sacrifices of the Covenanters
who had been persecuted severely during the reigns of Charles II
and his brother James. Roman Catholicism was outlawed and
Episcopalian ministers dismissed from their churches.

The leaders of the Church of Scotland believed very firmly in
predestination and that they were God's chosen people. The celebration of traditional festivals such as Christmas and May Day and the
staging of musical or theatrical performances were all strictly
forbidden. Local councils such as that in Edinburgh and even the law
courts were fearful of giving offence to the local presbytery of the
Church of Scotland. Through the local presbyteries and individual
Kirk Sessions the church authorities rigorously clamped down on
what they considered to be 'godless behaviour' and severely punished
offenders who in their eyes were guilty of sinning or blasphemy.

On 23 December 1696, an 18-year-old student Thomas Aitken-head had been tried for blasphemy accused of having been heard to say that Christianity was 'a rapsodie of feigned and ill-invented nonsense' and that 'Christianity would be extirpat by the year 1800.' At his trial at the High Court in Edinburgh, five witnesses claimed to have heard him say these things. No defence witnesses were allowed. Aitkenhead apologised, confirmed his belief in the scrip-tures and the Holy Trinity and promised to make amends. He was, however, unanimously found guilty and sentenced to death. Aitken-head appealed to the Privy Council where his case did find some support. However, the Privy Council ruled that they would not grant a reprieve unless the General Assembly of the Church of Scotland supported his appeal for mercy. But there was to be no mercy. The Assembly urged 'vigorous execution' to curb 'the abounding of impiety and profanity in this land'. Thus Aitkenhead was hanged outside Edinburgh on 8 January 1697 clutching a bible in his hand. He was the last person to be executed for blasphemy in the United Kingdom. Scotland was very much in an iron grip of repression and it took some courage to mount a challenge to the dominance of the Kirk. Two men who rose to that challenge were Allan Ramsay, the father of the portrait painter of the same name, and David Hume.

Allan Ramsay was born in 1686 at Leadhills in Lanarkshire, to John Ramsay, superintendent of Lord Hopetoun's lead-mines, and his wife, Alice Bower, a native of Derbyshire. He was educated at the parish school of Crawford, and in 1701 was apprenticed to a wig-maker in Edinburgh. In a few years he had established himself as a wig-maker (not as a barber, as has been often said) in the High Street, and soon found himself in comfortable circumstances. He married Christian Ross in 1712. They had six children. His eldest child was Allan Ramsay, the celebrated portrait painter. Ramsay's first efforts in verse-making were inspired by the meetings of the Easy Club (founded in 1712), of which he was an original member, and in 1715 he became the Club Laureate. Club members researched old Scots poetry which they shared with their fellow-members. For a bit of fun, members created names for themselves. Ramsay assumed the name of 'Isaac Bickerstaff', a pseudonym then being used by the writer Jonathan Swift. Later he took the name of 'Gawin [Gavin] Douglas', the famous 16th-century Bishop of Dunkeld who was also a poet. By 1718 Ramsay was publishing his own poems as broadsheets, which he displayed in his shop window in the High Street and sold to interested customers.

Soon (like John Kay some seventy years later) he decided to give up his normal day-job and opened up Edinburgh's first bookshop. In 1716 he had published an old Scots poem 'Christ's Kirk on the Green' from the *Bannatyne Manuscript*. The *Bannatyne Manuscript* was an important anthology of early Scots poetry which had been collected in the 16th century by George Bannatyne, an Edinburgh merchant. This included some of the works of the famous Scottish 'Makars', the court poets of James IV such as William Dunbar and Robert Henryson, whose work might otherwise have been lost. In the following year, Ramsay published some more poems from the anthology and added in some of his own compositions. He followed this up by publishing a collection of old Scots songs. The success of these ventures prompted him to collect his poems in 1722. The volume was issued by subscription, and brought in the sum of 400 guineas (£420).

Four years later he moved to another shop further up the High Street in the Luckenbooths in the shadow of St Giles. From his new premises, Ramsay created Edinburgh's first lending library in 1725. (The first in Scotland had been founded at Innerpeffray in Perthshire in 1680.) This immediately incurred the wrath of the Edinburgh Presbytery, who described Ramsay's library as follows:

> Profaneness is come to a great height! All the villainous, profane and obscene books are down from London by Allan Ramsay and let out for an easy price to young boys, servant women of the better sort and gentlemen and vice and obscenity dreadfully propagated.

The library, however, was proving to be very popular, and Ramsay had some very powerful supporters forcing the Presbytery to grudgingly back down. Ramsay had already challenged the grip of the Kirk on Scotland's social life by opening a Dancing Assembly at the top of the West Bow in 1710. The Edinburgh Presbytery forced the Council to close it down.

However, fashionable Edinburgh was determined not to lose the pleasure of an evening's dancing, so in 1720 a Dancing Assembly

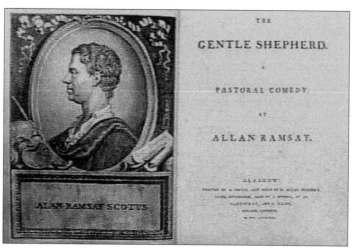

ABOVE. The title page of Allan Ramsay's *The Gentle Shepherd.*

OPPOSITE. The first Assembly Room at the top of the West Bow (James Skene, 1817).

was opened in the High Street in what is now Old Assembly Close. In 1756, a grander Assembly Room was opened in Bell's Close just further down the High Street – now known as New Assembly Close.

Between the publication of the collected edition of his poems and his settling down in the Luckenbooths, Ramsay had issued the first instalments of *The Tea-Table Miscellany* and *The Ever Green* between the years 1724 and 1727. *The Tea-Table Miscellany* was a collection of some of Ramsay's own work, some by his friends, and several well-known traditional ballads and songs. *The Ever Green* was a collection of older Scots verse and songs. Ramsay was inspired to collect these pieces and to preserve them for his contemporaries.

While engaged on these projects, Ramsay wrote his most famous work, *The Gentle Shepherd*, which was published in 1725. This, the first Scottish opera, was an immediate popular success and established Ramsay's reputation. The English writer John Gay drew heavily from *The Gentle Shepherd* for his famous production *The Beggars' Opera*, first performed in London in 1728.

Ramsay wrote little afterwards, though he published a few shorter poems, and new editions of his earlier work. By now his reputation had spread beyond Scotland. He wrote some prologues and epilogues for the London theatre and corresponded with a wide circle of literary friends including John Gay, who visited him in Edinburgh, and the poet Alexander Pope.

Ramsay had always been interested in the theatre but the opposition of the Kirk made public performances very difficult. In 1736 he set about the opening of a new theatre, 'at vast expense', in Carrubber's Close in Edinburgh's High Street. The Edinburgh Presbytery was outraged:

> A company of stage-players who are acting Plays within the precincts of the town have begun with acting one which is filled with horrid swearing, obscenity and expressions of double meaning.

Faced with this determined opposition, Ramsay was forced to close his theatre in 1737. Undeterred Edinburgh theatre-lovers tried again. A series of music concerts was organised to be held in The Tailors' Hall in the Cowgate. These concerts had extraordinarily long intervals during which short plays were performed to the delight of the audience but not to the Edinburgh Presbytery who again condemned the practice of theatre-going.

The solution for Ramsay and his supporters was, in 1747, to fund the opening of another new theatre but this time one in the separate burgh of the Canongate, beyond the influence of Edinburgh's Presbytery and Burgh Council. However, this new theatre was not without its problems which had nothing to do with the wrath of the Kirk.

The new Playhouse, located in the Old Playhouse Close in the Canongate, was managed by a London actor, Mr John Ryan. Performances were marred by frequent riots. In 1749, a group of English officers from the Castle loudly demanded that the orchestra play 'Culloden'. The orchestra instead, to cheers from the crowd, played 'You're Welcome Charlie Stewart'. Incensed, the officers drew their swords and attacked the orchestra. Other members of the audience rushed to protect the musicians including some Highland Sedan chairmen who hit the officers with their long poles and drove them from the theatre. Shortly after there was a pitched battle in the theatre between two rival groups each claiming ownership of the premises. Much damage was done and the theatre was set on fire. The building was repaired and opened again for business.

Perhaps the most famous evening's performance at the theatre

The Old Playhouse Close, the Canongate. The theatre was closed in 1769 when the Theatre Royal was opened in the New Town. John Kay did six portraits depicting performances at the Theatre Royal so he must have been a regular theatre-goer.

took place on 14 December 1756. The theatre was filled to over-flowing for the first performance of *Douglas*, a historical tragedy written by John Hume, Minister of Athelstaneford in East Lothian. This infuri-ated the Church already hostile to stage performances. The Presbytery of Edinburgh ordered ministers to preach a warning to all those who were thinking of attending what they described as 'The Temple of the Father of Lies'. Ministers bold enough to attend were threatened with suspension or even worse. The Reverend Alexander Carlyle of

Inveresk, our eyewitness of the Porteous Riot, was tried by the East
Lothian Presbytery for having attended a performance but the case
was dismissed on appeal to the General Assembly of the Church of
Scotland thanks to the intervention of some powerful friends. The
Reverend John Witherspoon condemned the play outright: 'A
dunghill covered in snow . . . a most unaccountable medley of
impiety, profaneness, error, immorality and vice.'

Witherspoon left Scotland in disgust at these moral failings. He
crossed the Atlantic; became Principal of Princeton College and was
a signatory of the American Declaration of Independence.

Despite the Kirk's opposition, the play was an immediate success
and played to packed houses. On the first night, one enthusiastic
member of the audience stood up and shouted at a group of army
officers from an English Regiment based at the Castle: 'Where's your
Wullie Shakespeare now?'

Hume was obliged to resign as a minister and moved to London
where *Douglas* was performed at Covent Garden with William Pitt
the Elder in the audience. Hume was awarded a pension of £100 a
year. He became Secretary to Lord Bute and a notable author. His
works included *A History of the Rebellion of 1745*. He retired to
Edinburgh but was badly injured by a fall from his horse, an injury
from which Hume never fully recovered. He died in 1808.

And what of Allan Ramsay? In 1755 he retired from his shop to
a house on the slope of the Castle Rock, still known as Ramsay
Lodge, which today forms part of the famous Ramsay Gardens. This
house was called by his friends 'The Goose-pie House', because of
its octagonal shape. Mrs Murray of Henderland, whose sister had
married the poet's son, remembered Allan Ramsay with great
affection as one of the most amiable men she had ever known.

> His constant cheerfulness and lively conversational powers
> made him a favourite amongst persons of rank whose guest
> he frequently was.

He delighted in playing with his grand-children, for whom he made
dolls, and entertaining his friends. Ramsay died in 1758. He is buried
in Greyfriars Kirkyard, Edinburgh. There is no gravestone to be seen
but a commemorative tablet was erected on the south side of the kirk.

One of Allan Ramsay's best friends was David Hume (see Plate

The statue of Allan Ramsay in Princes Street Gardens with the Goose-pie House in the background.

6), a man of towering intellect, who also successfully challenged the Kirk's grip on the nation. Hume was born in Edinburgh in 1711. He studied at Edinburgh University but did not graduate. Hume suffered from bouts of depression and was sent by his family to recover with relatives in Bristol where he worked as a counting-house clerk. Hume though had not abandoned his studies. He read voraciously and began to develop his philosophical theories.

Hume then travelled in France for three years and delighted in the intellectual atmosphere which he found in Paris. His first major work, *A Treatise of Human Nature*, was published anonymously in London in 1739. It was a challenging book to read and was a commercial failure. According to Hume: 'It fell dead-born from the press.' He was very disappointed. The book challenged the theories of 'Natural Law' (Thomas Hobbes) and the 'Social Contract' (John

Locke and Jean-Jacques Rousseau). He reworked his ideas and in 1741 he published the very popular *Essays Moral and Political.* Now a man in his thirties, Hume realised that there was no place for God or organised religion in his life. Hume argued that 'All religion is a work of the human imagination', and warned against what he saw as the dangers of 'transcendent religious preaching'. This was a brave decision to take as it effectively closed the doors to an academic appointment. Hume's atheism excluded him from posts in Moral Philosophy at Glasgow and Edinburgh Universities as at both institutions the Kirk had a major say in academic appointments. Instead in 1745 he travelled in Europe as a Tutor to the insane Marquis of Annandale. Hume was thus absent from Edinburgh when it was captured by the Jacobites in September of that year.

Hume then worked as a diplomat for the British Government, who were keen to make use of his wide range of influential contacts in Europe. However, he missed Edinburgh and his wide circle of friends. Influence was brought to bear and in 1752 Hume was appointed Keeper of the Signet Library in Edinburgh. This post gave him time to devote to his writing. Other works now flowed from his pen: *An Enquiry Concerning Human Understanding* was published in 1748; *Political Discourses* in 1752 and his hugely popular five-volume *History of England* between 1754 and 1767.

Hume now began to take a leading role in the growing intellectual life of Edinburgh. The Select Society of Edinburgh held its first meeting in the Advocates' Library on 22 May 1754 attended by Allan Ramsay, David Hume, Adam Smith, John Home, William Robertson, Alexander Carlyle and Professors Munro and Hope. Twenty-one years' old Alexander Wedderburn (future Lord Chancellor in the House of Lords) was elected President. Matters debated included 'Whether ought we to prefer ancient or modern manners with regard to the condition and treatment of women?'; 'Whether the difference in national character be chiefly owing to the nature of different climates or to moral and political issues?' and 'The happiest marriages are found where love by every acquaintance is consolidated into friendship.'

Encouraged by his growing reputation as a leading thinker, Hume now launched a full-frontal assault on religious fanaticism. In *An Enquiry Concerning Human Understanding,* Hume had argued that 'So that on the whole, we may conclude, that the Christian

Religion not only was first attended with miracles, but even at this day cannot be believed by any reasonable person without one.' For Hume 'Belief is a feeling rather than a rational process.'

This was too much of a challenge for the Kirk to ignore. The General Assemblies of 1755 and 1756 sought to try David Hume and his friend Henry Home (the future Lord Kames) on the grounds of 'infidelity'. There were six specific charges brought against the two men. Charge Number Four 'Religion and its ministers are prejudicial to mankind and will always be found either to run into the heights of superstition or enthusiasm' and Charge Number Five 'Christianity has no evidence of being a divine revelation' were seen as the most serious. Both men, however, had the support of many powerful friends. The cases were thrown out much to the embarrassment of the Kirk and the delight of their friends. One such friend of the two men, John Ramsay of Ochtertyre, noted:

> The two culprits were more caressed and admired than ever and by none more than the moderate clergy . . . In a word this rash and feeble attempt to check the progress of freethinking convinced the philosophers of Edinburgh that they had no longer anything to dread from the Church Courts.

Hume was now something of an international celebrity. Between 1763 and 1765 he worked as Secretary to the British Ambassador in Paris. Here he was welcomed into French literary and academic circles. He delighted in the company of the French 'philosophes'. 'Here I feed on ambrosia, drink nothing but nectar, breathe incense only and walk on flowers.' In 1767 he was appointed as Under-Secretary of State for the Northern Department which covered the North of England and the whole of Scotland. In 1768 he returned to Edinburgh where he became the centre of the town's own literary and academic circle. Hume was a confirmed bachelor and an excellent cook. He first took up residence in Riddle's Court on the south side of the Lawnmarket. Riddle's Court had been built in 1726 by George Riddle a successful Edinburgh merchant. The Court offered upmarket apartments to wealthier citizens. Hume moved across the road to James Court in 1762. From there he moved in 1771 to take up lodgings in St David's Street, one of the first houses to be built in Edinburgh's New Town.

WHAL O CALLER OYSTERS

A Newhaven fishwife, drawn by John Kay.

An amusing story of David Hume tells of how he was keen to see the progress being made with his new home in the New Town. With the North Bridge being repaired, Hume left his Old Town apartment in James Court and took a short-cut across the partially drained Nor' Loch. He slipped and fell in. Hume was rather heavily built and struggled to get out. He had to be pulled free of the mud

The David Hume Mausoleum in the Old Calton Burial Ground.

by two Newhaven fishwives who would only help him if he would recite the Lord's Prayer – which he did.

Hume's remaining years were spent in the company of his friends. He encouraged them to look critically at the world around them and to search empirically for rational explanations of what they saw. The only discordant note occurred in 1773, when Dr Samuel Johnson arrived in Edinburgh at the invitation of James Boswell who had moved into Hume's old apartment in James Court. Johnson received all the leading Edinburgh intellectuals of the day apart from Hume, whom he refused to meet because of his atheism. Hume's last days were spent in his home in St David's Street. He knew that he was dying and encouraged his friends to come to say their farewells. Among his visitors was James Boswell who recorded in his dairy his astonishment that a man as clever as Hume could go peacefully to his grave without acknowledging that there was a God in the hope of saving his soul. Hume told Boswell that he sincerely believed it a 'most unreasonable fancy' that there might be life after death.

David Hume died on 25 August 1776. He was buried in the Old Calton Burial Ground in Edinburgh. His great friend Adam Smith the economist arranged for a mausoleum to be erected in his memory.

CHAPTER 5

'A Picturesque, Odorous, Inconvenient, Old-fashioned Town'

In 1825, literary Edinburgh was astonished at the publication of *The Traditions of Edinburgh.* They were even more astonished when it was revealed that the author of the best-selling book, Robert Chambers, was only twenty-two years old. Young Robert Chambers and his brother William had come from Peebles with their family when their father was forced into bankruptcy. While William started his own publishing business, Robert opened a bookstall selling off some of his father's books.

Robert Chambers.

He was very conscious that great changes were afoot in Edinburgh as most of the better-off citizens had abandoned the historic Old Town for the spacious houses of the developing New Town and the expanding suburbs to the south. He decided to 'walk' his readers down the ancient Royal Mile capturing the stories of the old buildings and the people who had lived in them before they were lost forever. For all those with a love for the history of Edinburgh, his book remains a classic.

Robert Chambers starts his 'walk' with the definitive description of Edinburgh's historic Old Town in 1760 on the eve of the start of the building programme that was to transform the city. It is worth quoting from his introduction to set the scene because the sights and sounds so wonderfully captured by Chambers must have been those experienced by young John Kay when he arrived in 1762.

Edinburgh was, at the beginning of George III's reign [1760], a picturesque, odorous, inconvenient, old-fashioned town, of about seventy thousand inhabitants . . . A stranger approaching the city, seeing it piled 'close and massy, deep and high' – a series of towers, rising from a palace of the plain to a castle in the air – would have thought it a truly romantic place; and the impression would not have subsided much on a near inspection, when he would have found himself admitted by a fortified gate [The Netherbow Port – demolished in 1764] through an ancient wall, still kept in repair . . .

Every forenoon, for several hours, the only clear space which the town presented – that around the Cross [the ancient Mercat Cross was demolished in 1756 but for many years Edinburgh folk, by force of habit, still gathered around the site of the Cross] – was crowded with loungers of all ranks . . . The jostle and huddlement was extreme everywhere. Gentlemen and ladies paraded along in the stately attire of the period; tradesmen chatted in groups, often bareheaded at their shop-doors; caddies [licensed messengers] whisked about, bearing messages or attending to the affairs of strangers; children filled the kennel with their noisy sports. Add to all this, corduroyed men from Gilmerton, bawling coals or yellow sand . . . fishwomen crying their caller haddies [fresh haddock] from Newhaven [a local

fishing port on the Firth of Forth]; whimsicals and idiots going along each with his or her crowd of listeners or tormentors; sootymen [chimneysweeps] with their bags; town-guardsmen with their antique Lochaber axes; water-carriers with their dripping barrels; barbers with their hair-dressing materials; and so forth – and our stranger would have been disposed to acknowledge that, though a coarse and confused, it was a perfectly unique scene, and one which, once contemplated, was not easily to be forgotten.

(Robert Chambers, *Traditions of Edinburgh*,
W. & C. Tait, Edinburgh, 1825)

The Edinburgh of the 1760s was indeed an overcrowded, smelly burgh of some 60,000 citizens. The 18th century had seen a surge in the burgh's population due in part to changes in Scottish farming which saw the start of the enclosure of the old run-rig system of land-holding together with innovations in farming methods. These saw increases in food production with an improvement in diet and the lessening of the threat of starvation which had caused the deaths of hundreds at the end of the 17th century. There was now a steady increase in Edinburgh's population as can be seen below:

1722   40,420 inhabitants
1755   57,195 inhabitants
1775   70,430 inhabitants
1791   84,886 inhabitants

For centuries this growing population had sheltered within the ancient town walls in the brooding shadow of Edinburgh Castle. Running eastwards from the Castle was the old medieval street which was in three unbroken sections. Starting at the foot of the approach to the Castle was the Castlehill which ran to the Weigh-House or Butter Tron at the head of the West Bow, the steep, winding approach to the Old Town from the Grassmarket below. Then came the Lawnmarket which ran into the High Street itself which ended at the Netherbow Port. Beyond its fortified towers

OPPOSITE. The Mercat Cross in the High Street (by James Riddel from the 1912 edition of *Traditions of Edinburgh*).

stretched the separate burgh of the Canongate that ended at the deserted Palace of Holyrood and the ruins of the 12th-century Abbey. Branching off to the north and south of the Royal Mile were some eighty narrow closes and wynds.

A remarkable feature of Edinburgh life was that all social classes mingled together and even lived on top of each other in the towering tenements which were a feature of the architecture of the historic Old Town. Unless you were very wealthy and could afford your own house set away from the High Street in its own courtyard or one of the expensive apartments in the open-courtyard developments such as James Court or Riddle's Court, both in the Lawnmarket, then you would find yourself with a very interesting social mix of near neighbours. Here is an example of this 'social mix' taken from a survey conducted in 1765:

Residents of Dickson's Close 1765
David Aitkenhead (Surgeon)
The Countess of Balcarres
George Buchan (Writer – a Lawyer)
Thomas Hay (Baxter – a Baker)
Mrs Murray (at 'The Mermaid' – an Edinburgh tavern)
Mrs Douglas
Provost George Drummond (Excise)
Thomas Fordyce (Writer)
William Watson (Ale Seller)
Robert Swan (Ale Seller)
Mr Rose (Painter)
Mr Hogg (Schoolmaster)
David Stark (Weaver)
George Syme (Slater)
Francis Kemptie (Merchant)
James Aitkenhead (Cordiner – a Leatherworker)

As you can see, the residents of this Close included a titled noble-woman, the Lord Provost of Edinburgh, a lawyer, surgeon, a publican, a teacher and several quite humble tradesmen and shop-keepers.

Fire was an ever present danger. This is part of a report of a fire at Old Bank Close, on the site of the present-day George IV Bridge:

On Saturday January 26th [1777] between 5 and 6 o'clock at night, a fire broke out in the garret storey of Buchanan's tenement at the head of the Old Bank Close [the Lawnmarket]. It was discovered by the flames bursting through the roof and at first seemed to threaten destruction to all that quarter of the city. It was not entirely quenched till Sunday morning about 8 o'clock.

The houses that suffered on this melancholy occasion [two citizens had perished fighting the flames] were possessed as follows: the shops of Messrs Dalgleish and Henderson, grocers and Mr. Ronaldson, baker; the 1st storey, by General Lockhart of Carnwath, the 2nd storey by Mrs. Porterfield; the 3rd by Mr. Ilay Campbell, advocate; the 4th. by Mr John Bell, W.S. [Writer to the Signet – a lawyer]; the 5th. by John Hume esq. of Ninewells, and the garret, where the fire began by General Lockhart's servants to whose carelessness the catastrophe is imputed.

Once again this illustrates the social mix that was such a feature of Old Town life. Interestingly the advocate Ilay Campbell, whose home was damaged in the fire, was to be one of the prosecuting counsel at the trial of Deacon William Brodie and his fellow-accused George Smith in 1788 which we will explore in chapter 14. Visitors and new arrivals such as John Kay were always impressed by the width of the Royal Mile and the height of the stone-built houses. Daniel Defoe made several visits to the city. He has left us a very full description in his *A Tour of the Whole of Great Britain and Ireland* published in three volumes between 1724 and 1726. This extract confirms the amazing height that some of these tenements had reached by the 18th century.

From the Palace west, the street goes on in almost a straight line and for near a mile and a half in length ... through the whole city to the castle ... this is perhaps, the largest, longest, and finest street for buildings and number of inhabitants, not in Britain only, but in the world ... The main street ... is the most spacious, the longest and best inhabited street in Europe ... its buildings are surprising both for strength and beauty, and for height, all or the greatest part of freestone,

and so firm is everything made, that though in so high a
situation, and in a country where storms and violent winds
are so frequent, 'tis rare that any damage is done here ... but
all is fixed and strong to the top, though you have in that
part of the city called the Parliament Close, houses which,
on the south side appear to be eleven or twelve storey high,
and inhabited to the very top'.

While praising the appearance of the Royal Mile, Defoe also
confirmed one of the less-pleasant experiences of other visitors to
the city:

> ... the city suffers infinite disadvantages, and lies under such
> scandalous inconveniences as are, by its enemies, made a
> subject of scorn and reproach, as if the people were not
> willing to live as sweet and clean as other nations, but
> delighted in stench and nastiness ... thronged buildings
> from seven to ten or twelve story high, a scarcity of water,
> and that little they have difficult to be had, and to the
> uttermost lodgings, far to fetch ... I believe, this may be said
> with truth, that in no city in the world so many people live
> in so little room as at Edinburgh.

Another English visitor, Joseph Taylor, recorded that:

> Every street shows the nastiness of the inhabitants; the
> excrement lies in heaps. The smell was so bad we were
> forced to hold our noses, and to take care where we stepped.
> We had to walk in the middle of the streets for fear of an
> accident on our heads. Our lodgings were as nasty as the
> streets and every room is scented with a close-stool
> [chamber pot]. All the family sleeps on the floor like pigs.
> There is an itch which is common among them. We have
> the best lodgings but it looks out on a place called 'the close'.
> It is a common thing for men and women to go into these
> closes to ease nature.

OPPOSITE. The top of the Lawnmarket.

James Court.

Another visitor who experienced the unpleasantness of living in Edinburgh was Captain Edward Burt, a British Army officer. Like many visitors, he was very impressed by the High Street. In a letter dated 1734 Burt wrote:

> When I first came into the High Street of that City I had not seen anything of the kind more magnificent, the extreme height of the houses; the breadth and length of the street. I was extremely pleased.'

However, he had a narrow escape on his way back to his lodgings:

We supped very plentifully . . . and were very merry till the clock struck ten, the hour when everybody is at liberty . . . to throw their filth out at the windows. The company then began to light pieces of paper . . . to smoke the room, and as I thought, to mix one bad smell with another. [Having] to pass to my lodgings, a guide was assigned to me, who went before me to prevent my disgrace . . . The opening of a window made me tremble, while behind and before me . . . fell the terrible shower.

To be fair, successive Councils had passed Acts forbidding the practice of householders just tipping their waste out of their tenement windows onto the streets below – but these were ignored. Folk would open their windows and cry 'Gardyloo!' taken from the French 'Watch out for the water!' – though of course more than water was being tipped out. David Hume and James Boswell lived in James Court on the north side of the Lawnmarket. James Court had been built by James Brownhill between 1723 and 1727. This was like Riddle's Court, an upmarket residential courtyard development designed to attract wealthier tenants eager to get away from the noise and smells of the streets. There was also the issue of having to share a common close and perhaps a common stair with 'the lower orders'.

Those able to afford the high rents of James Court had to follow very strict regulations. In 1786 the 1st Regulation stated that: 'No person shall at any time throw out, from any window or door in the Court, any water, ashes, or nastiness of any kind.'

Of course it was not just the problem of human waste that folk had to contend with. There was the waste deposited by the hundreds of horses required for a population of some 60,000. Added to this was the waste left behind by the hundreds of cattle, poultry and sheep that were regularly being driven to the shambles situated on the side of the Nor' Loch at the foot of Fleshmarket Close.

The Edinburgh that greeted John Kay and his young family in 1762 was indeed an overcrowded, noisy and extremely smelly city. However, there was one man determined to improve the appearance and quality of life of his adopted home. This man was Lord Provost George Drummond.

CHAPTER 6

Dreams of a New Town

Writing around the year 1773, the Reverend Thomas Somerville recalled a conversation that he had with Lord Provost George Drummond some thirty years before.

> I happened one day to be standing at a window looking out to the opposite side of the Nor' Loch, then called Bearford's Park, in which there was not a single house to be seen. 'Look at these fields,' says Provost Drummond. 'You Mr Somerville are a young man and may probably live, though I will not, to see all these fields covered with houses, forming a splendid and magnificent city. To the accomplishment of this nothing more is necessary than draining the Nor' Loch and providing a proper access from the Old Town. I have never lost sight of this object since the year 1725 when I was first elected Provost.'

Edinburgh has been fortunate in having had several inspirational Lord Provosts. There can be few though whose achievements can match those of George Drummond (see Plate 7). As well as being the driving-force for Edinburgh's New Town, he was also the man who persuaded his fellow citizens to put their hands in their pockets to fund the burgh's Royal Infirmary and the Royal Exchange, now the City Chambers.

George Drummond was not a native of Edinburgh. He was born in Perthshire in 1687. He came to Edinburgh to complete his

education and took up a job in the Excise Office. He proved to be a
very able employee and in 1707 was appointed as the Accountant
General. He gained further promotion in 1715 when he was
appointed as Scotland's Commissioner of Customs at the huge
salary of £1,000 a year (about £135,000 today). However, his work
was interrupted with the start of the 1715 Jacobite Rebellion. Drummond joined the army of the Duke of Argyll and fought against the
Jacobites at the Battle of Sheriffmuir which took place outside
Dunblane in Perthshire. Although the government forces of Argyll
were outnumbered, the battle was inconclusive. The Jacobites had
lost momentum and the rebellion petered out.

It will be recalled that Drummond was also the commander of
the Edinburgh Volunteers; the citizen force hurriedly assembled in
what proved to be a futile attempt to defend the burgh from Bonnie
Prince Charlie's Jacobites in September 1745.

Drummond was first elected as Lord Provost in 1725. Uniquely,
he was elected as Lord Provost on five further occasions – 1746, 1750,
1754, 1758 and finally, at the age of 75, in 1762.

In 1736, Drummond persuaded his fellow citizens to subscribe
to the construction of a proper hospital – the Royal Infirmary.
Edinburgh citizens supported the project with great enthusiasm.
Those who could not donate money were encouraged to give

Drummond's Royal Infirmary from the north (John Elphinstone, 1745).

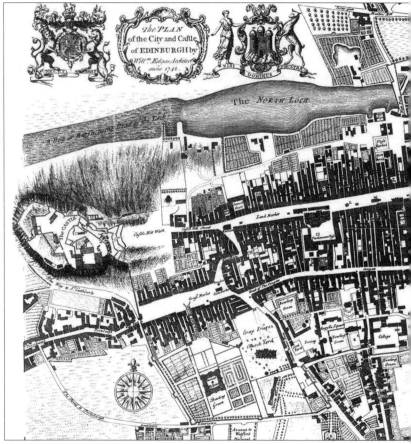

Edgar's Map of Edinburgh 1742 shows the classic Old Town on the eve of work starting on the building of the New Town.

materials or even their labour. Amongst the first subscribers was the ill-fated Captain John Porteous, Commander of the Town Guard, who just a few weeks later was to meet a miserable end hanging from a barber's pole in the Grassmarket.

Work got underway in 1738 and was finally completed in 1745 when seventy patients were admitted. The famous Scottish architect William Adam (father of the better-known architects Robert and John Adam) was responsible for the project. To save money, Adam adapted a plan for a military barracks. The building was demolished in 1873.

Drummond next turned his energies towards taking forward

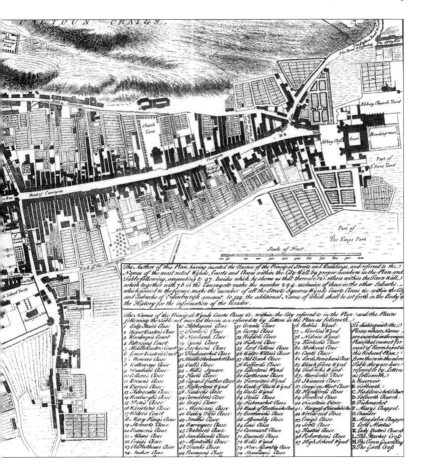

his dream of what even then was called Edinburgh's New Town. First the Council had to obtain Parliament's and the King's permission to extend the historic royalty of the burgh. This was required to ensure that the burgh had jurisdiction over any future building works that went beyond the existing boundaries.

Drummond established a committee to prepare a report arguing the case for Edinburgh's development, which was to be presented to Parliament. The committee published its report *Proposals for Carrying on Certain Public Works in the City of Edinburgh* on 8 July 1752. The actual authorship of the report is not given but clearly Drummond must have played a major part in its completion.

The report introduces its proposals with a hard-hitting critique of Edinburgh's situation, particularly when compared with 'the delightful prospect which LONDON affords . . .'

Placed upon the ridge of a hill, it admits but of one good street, running from east to west; and even this is only tolerably accessible only from one quarter. The narrow lanes leading to the north and south, by reason of their steepness, narrowness and dirtiness, can only be considered as so many avoidable nuisances. Confined by the compass of the walls, and the narrow limits of the royalty, which scarcely extends beyond the walls, the houses stand more crowded than in any other town in Europe, and are built to a height that is almost incredible. Hence necessarily follows a great want of free air, light, cleanliness, and every other comfortable accommodation. Hence also many families, sometimes no less than ten or a dozen, are obliged to live overhead of each other in the same building; where to all the other inconveniences, is added that of a common stair, which is no other in effect than an upright street, constantly dark and dirty. It is owing to the same narrowness of situation, that the principal street [the High Street] is encumbered with the herb-market, the fruit-market, and several others; that the shambles [the butchers' slaughter houses] are placed upon the side of the North-Loch, rendering what was originally an ornament of the town, a most insufferable nuisance. No less observable is the great deficiency of public buildings . . . There is no exchange for our merchants, no safe repository for our public and private records; no place of meeting for our magistrates and town council . . . To such reasons alone it must be imputed that EDINBURGH, which ought to have set the first example of industry and improvement, is the last of our trading cities that has shook off the unaccountable supineness [lethargy] which has so long and so fatally depressed the spirit of this nation . . .

A committee comprising leading members of the Council and the judiciary was charged to take the proposals forward. This was to prove to be a long and drawn-out task. It was not until 1767, five

The Royal Exchange, now the City Chambers, with the 1885 Mercat Cross in the foreground.

years after John Kay had moved to Edinburgh, that an Act of Parliament finally granted permission to extend the royalty of the burgh.

Drummond had not been idle. One of the proposals for improvement had been to follow the lead of London and to build an Exchange for Edinburgh's merchants who up until then had tended to conduct their business around the Mercat Cross in the High Street or in one of Edinburgh's many taverns. Drummond was determined to end this and in 1756 had the old Cross demolished.

Once again he asked his fellow-citizens to help to raise the money to improve their city. Work started on preparing the foundations of what was to be Edinburgh's Royal Exchange in 1753. The project was again designed by William Adam, the architect of the Royal Infirmary. Several old closes were demolished on the north side of the High Street to make way for the Exchange. Among them was Mary King's Close which had been abandoned in 1645 after the last serious outbreak of the plague. Much of the spoil from these demolished buildings was used to construct the Esplanade of Edinburgh Castle.

The Royal Exchange complete with offices, a large meeting hall and a coffee shop was opened for business in 1761. However, it was a commercial failure. The Edinburgh merchants much preferred to carry on their traditional ways of doing business, so the Exchange was largely ignored. In his popular novel *Humphrey Clinker* written in Edinburgh and published in 1766, author Tobias Smollet remarks that:

> All the people of business in Edinburgh, and even the genteel company, may be seen standing in crowds every day from one to two in the afternoon at the site of the Cross as a force of custom, rather than move a few yards to an Exchange that stands empty on one side

The Exchange was taken over by the Council as their headquarters in 1811.

In 1761 a private developer, James Brown, purchased land from the Ross Estate just to the south of Edinburgh and built a small residential square which he named after his brother George. The attractive George Square proved to be a very popular development and the houses were quickly sold to some of Edinburgh's better-off families keen to get away from all the unpleasant inconveniences of the Old Town.

The success of this piece of private enterprise spurred Drummond on. In 1763 work started on draining the eastern end of the Nor' Loch. In anticipation that at long last Parliament was going to grant permission for the burgh's royalty to be extended, he announced a competition inviting plans to be submitted to develop the open lands beyond the Nor' Loch. The competition was advertised in April 1766.

Interested parties were only given a month to submit their plans. When entries closed on 21 May, there were six submissions. In June, Entry Number four was declared to be the winner. This was the plan submitted by a young, unknown architect James Craig (see Plate 8), who was only twenty-six years old.

At the insistence of King George III, this New Town was to be a celebration of Great Britain and the royal house of Hanover. The

Houses on George Square, a popular residential development in the late 1700s.

principal street, running along a natural ridge of higher ground was to be named George Street after the King himself and his son the Prince of Wales. Hanover Street celebrated the King's family name and Frederick Street was named after his father who had died in 1751.

The original plan shown to George III had the southern street, in the shadow of the Castle and the Old Town, named 'St Giles Street' after Edinburgh's patron saint. King George was not best pleased with this suggestion. He is reported to have stamped his feet and shouted: 'Hey! Hey! What! What! St Giles Street! Never do! Never do!'

The King was not being anti-Edinburgh or anti-Scottish. St Giles was also the patron saint of lepers and beggars, and the district of St Giles in London was a hotbed of crime and loose living. So the name was changed to Princes Street after the King's two young sons, George and Frederick. The two squares were to be named after the patron saints of Scotland (St Andrew) and England (St George).

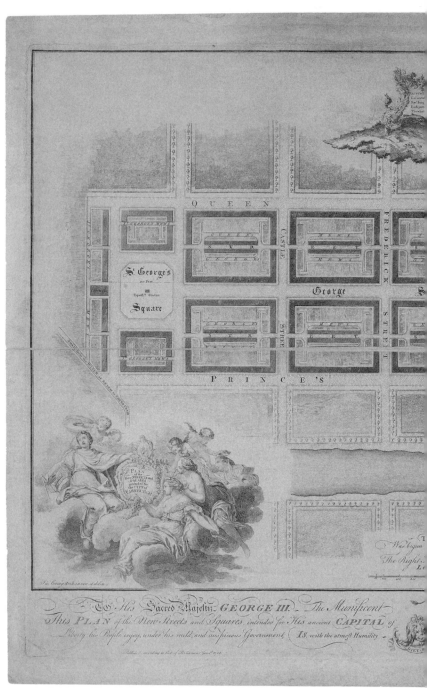

James Craig's New Town Plan, 1767.

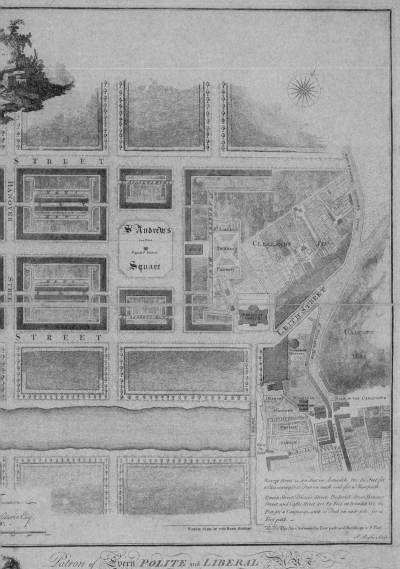

HANOVER STREET

STREET

STREET

St Andrew's
100 Feet
Equestr? Statue
Square

CHURCH

S.T LAURENCE

DUNDAS

PROPERTY

CLELLANDS FEU

LEITH STREET

CALTOUN
HILL

BACK OF THE CANONGATE

ORPHAN HOSPITAL

GROUNDS

PRECINCT

GAMBLE
ROAD IS IRREGULAR

NORTH SIDE OF THE HIGH STREET

George Street is 100 Feet in Breadth, 12 & 65 Feet for
a Causeway, & 20 Feet on each side for a Foot path.

Queen Street, Prince's Street, Frederick Street, Hanover
Street, and Castle Street are 80 Feet in Breadth 1/2, 60
Feet for a Causeway, and 10 Feet on each side, for a
Foot path.

☞ The Area between the Foot path and Buildings is 8 Feet

J. Ryder Sculp

Patron of Every POLITE and LIBERAL
NORTH BRITAIN; One of the happy Consequences of the Peace, Security, and
Inscribed By   His Majesty's   Most devoted Servant and Subject
JAMES CRAIG

1 Thistle Court, the first house built in the New Town.

Unfortunately there already was a George Square in Edinburgh so the western square was instead named after George's wife and his eldest daughter, both called Charlotte.

The plan was finally accepted in July 1767, and in August of that year Craig laid the foundation stone of the first house built in the New Town, which still stands in Thistle Court.

George Drummond unfortunately did not live to see work starting on his New Town. His last public act was to lay the founda-

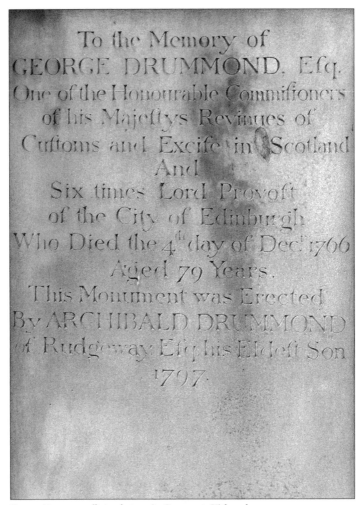

George Drummond's tombstone in Canongate Kirkyard.

tion stone for the connecting North Bridge in October 1765 over the partially drained Nor' Loch. He died in December 1766 and is buried in the Canongate Kirkyard.

He was a remarkable man in so many ways. In addition to taking forward his ideas to improve his adopted city, he had also supported improvements at Edinburgh University's medical school. He was married four times and was the father of fourteen children.

CHAPTER 7

A Change of
Careers

In 1771, at the age of twenty-nine, Kay became a member of Edinburgh's Society of Surgeon-Barbers, paying the considerable sum of £40 (about £5,000 today) for this privilege as he was not a citizen of Edinburgh. Kay rented a small workshop for himself on the south side of Parliament Close. He was now ready to welcome his first customers.

The first entry for Kay in the Post Office Directory is in 1776: 'John Kay, hairdresser, above the Guard [The Town Guardhouse], in the High Street, North Side'. Several High Street addresses follow before he settled in Parliament Square 1807–1813. From 1814 to 1820, he is recorded as a 'Printseller' residing at 243 High Street. In 1823 he moved for a year to 73 Princes Street and then spent the last three years of his life at 227 High Street.

Kay worked very successfully as a barber for several years. He seems to have had a particular talent for dressing gentlemen's wigs for which he charged 4 guineas (£4.20) and appears to have had no shortage of customers. Several members of the aristocracy and the landed gentry patronised his shop.

Alexander Kincaid's 1784 plan shows St Giles' Kirk with Parliament Close beneath it to the south. Kay's workshop was in the middle of the south side of the Close. The plan also shows the Royal Exchange on the north side of the High Street. Kay's house No. 227 was just to the right [eastwards] of the Exchange. From his shop window, Kay could look past the equestrian statue of Charles II to St Giles' Kirk and the little stalls that had attached themselves to the

Kincaid's Plan of 1784 showing St Giles' Kirk and Parliament Close.

side of the medieval kirk. To his left was the Parliament Hall, where the Scottish Parliament had voted itself out of existence when agreeing to the Act of Union in 1707. Another near neighbour was the bank of Sir William Forbes of Pitsligo, soon to be one of Kay's subjects.

As we know from his biographical note quoted earlier, Kay had a natural artistic talent. As a child he delighted in drawing. We are told that he liked to sketch some of his customers and to display his drawings in his shop window. Sometimes a small crowd would gather to admire them, curious to see who was the latest Edinburgh worthy to be caricatured by Kay. Perhaps he was offered money for the purchase of one of them and this was the encouragement that he needed to consider a change of career? Or perhaps it was the support that Kay received from one of his better-off customers, Mr William Nisbet of Archerfield House, Dirleton. He regularly invited Kay to his home in East Lothian to cut and dress the hair of family members. It was at Archerfield that Kay was encouraged by Mr Nisbet, who bought him crayons, paints and brushes, to develop his skill as an artist. It is believed that Kay sketched and drew miniature portraits of several members of the Nisbet family.

He also experimented in portrait painting in oils, including a rare surviving self-portrait (see Plate 1). Yet John Kay was no schooled artist. Unlike his contemporaries Allan Ramsay, Sir Henry Raeburn, Alexander Nasmyth and Sir David Wilkie, he received no formal instruction. It must have been apparent to Kay that he could never hope to compete with artists who had benefited from such professional training. Instead he concentrated on developing his talents as a caricature artist. Furthermore he seems also to have taught himself the skills of engraving.

Kay became a close friend of Mr Nisbet's and regularly accompanied him on his travels. Conscious that Kay's business was being neglected, Mr Nisbet gave him an allowance. However, Mr Nisbet died in 1783. His son, appreciating the friendship that his father had enjoyed with Kay, gave him an annuity of £20 a year.

At the start of his book *An Account of the Trial of George Smith and William Brodie before the High Court of Justiciary on the 27th and 28th days of August 1788*, William Creech, the Edinburgh bookseller and publisher, included a note about John Kay, who had provided two engravings – one of Deacon Brodie in the condemned cell in the Tolbooth and one of George Smith at the bar in the High Court of Edinburgh. Creech largely confirms the information provided later by Kay in his biographical note published posthumously in 1837. Presumably this information would almost certainly have been provided by Kay himself? What is particularly interesting is what Creech has to say concerning Kay's methods of working and the impressive number of portraits completed in such a short space of time.

> John Kay forced himself on the attention of the public in Edinburgh, by the efforts of his genius; which, although at first rude, showed that if his talent had been cultivated, he might have risen to excellence . . .
>
> When a very young boy he discovered the bent of his genius by drawing figures with pieces of burnt sticks. That dawning of genius, unhappily for him however, was not marked by any kind patron; and in his lot he enjoyed no means of cultivating his talents. The shaving of beards and the dressing of wigs for Sunday, he did not much relish, and left his apprenticeship. His mother beat him, and sent him back to his master, with whom he served out his six years. He had then nothing to depend upon but his diligence in his profession. In the course of his vacation he fell in with the late Mr Nisbet of Dirleton, who took a liking to him from having discovered his talents, and kept Kay much about him, although flattering, yet lost him his other customers.
>
> In this situation he had some leisure time, and the bent

of his genius again showed itself . . . he drew several single figures and groups, which attracted much attention, all of them being done from transient observations. The likenesses he struck upon many occasions, and often from a single glance, astonished the public. Without a lesson in drawing, etching or engraving, he has, since Mr Nisbet's death a few years since, taught himself all these arts. The sale of these etchings, which are now above a hundred, enable him to prosecute his favourite propensity; and he has lately begun to miniature painting, in which with study, he must excel, for the likenesses he makes from a single view, or from memory, are altogether astonishing. He is now a man about forty with a wife and family.

How did Kay work? How did he compose his portraits? Creech suggests that Kay had almost a photographic memory and that he could catch the image of his subjects 'often from a single glance'. This would suggest that Kay used his workshop in Parliament Close for the completion of his drawings and the engraving process – not as a studio. You can then imagine Kay with pencil and sketch book in hand walking the streets of Edinburgh searching for suitable subjects to draw. One of his most charming characters is the study of Robert Craig of Riccarton sitting outside his house, No. 91 Princes Street, enjoying the early morning sun (see overleaf).

Craig is dressed wearing his favourite broad-brimmed hat and holding his long walking staff. Watching him from the front window is his servant William Scott who served Craig for some forty years. Craig sat outside his front door for many years enjoying the fresh air and greeting passers-by. Whenever he needed assistance from his servant he would blow a whistle which he kept in his pocket. Craig died in 1823 at the advanced age of ninety-three. It is easy to imagine Kay standing on the pavement of Princes Street catching Craig in this typical pose.

So it is safe to assume that much of Kay's preliminary work was done on the streets of Edinburgh. Doubtless some characters would just catch his eye as he went on his walks, but others, perhaps interesting visitors to Edinburgh, he would seek out and make his preliminary sketches.

Most of Kay's characters are indeed drawn walking on the streets

of Edinburgh; several are shown crossing the North Bridge. The majority of his portraits are drawn in profile. As we shall see, however, some of his better-known characters would appear to be posing perhaps in their homes or in their places of work. For example, the infamous Deacon William Brodie is shown posing in the condemned cell of the burgh's Tolbooth. (See page 174.)

Kay's output is hugely impressive. Creech notes that in 1788, just four years after his first commercially-produced portrait, he had already produced 'now above a hundred [of these etchings]'. Some authorities credit Kay with publishing 900 of these portraits. This equates to some thirty portraits a year from 1784 to about 1822 when he completed his last portrait, possibly that of Archibald Campbell, the City Officer. (See page 229.)

If Kay's own account is to be believed, he was forty-six in 1788. His first wife Lily Steven, whom he had married when he was only nineteen years old, had died in 1785. (There are no entries in the Old Parish Registers to confirm either their marriage or the death of Lily Steven.) She had borne him ten children. Nine of these children died in infancy. Only William survived into adulthood but he too predeceased his father. Such dreadful infant mortality was sadly all too common. Six of Walter Scott's eleven brothers and sisters died as children.

Perhaps it was the death of his first wife which prompted Kay to give up his career as a barber and wigmaker and to try to earn his living as an artist. Or perhaps it was the growing interest being taken in the prints that he was now displaying in his shop-window. Whatever the reason for this bold step, it is believed that the print overleaf, *Dr Glen and the Daft Highland Laird,* was the first that he sold commercially. Kay normally initialled and dated his portraits. This one is dated 1784. This is confirmed by Robert Chambers in his entry for John Kay in his *Scottish Biographical Dictionary.*

> In 1784 he [Kay] published his first caricature, which repre-
> sented a half-crazed Jacobite gentleman, named Laird
> Robertson, who was wont to amuse the citizens of Edin-
> burgh by cutting caricatured resemblances of public charac-
> ters who he fixed on the head of his stick . . .

OPPOSITE. Robert Craig of Riccarton c.1788.

John Kay, *Dr Glen and the Daft Highland Laird.*

Dr Glen, on the left, was well into his seventies when Kay sketched him. He had earned a fortune abroad and had retired back to Edinburgh. However, he had a reputation for being very tight with his money. It was even claimed that on the death of his first wife he had advertised for a second-hand coffin. Dr Glen seems to have been very much a man for the ladies. Despite his advanced years he arrived in Edinburgh determined to marry again. He courted a much younger woman and promised her a fine new carriage if she would accept his hand in marriage. The young lady agreed and the couple were married. The new Mrs Glen eagerly awaited the promised carriage. The carriage was duly delivered – but without any horses to pull it. She challenged Dr Glen on what she saw as a broken promise. He is reputed to have replied 'I promised a carriage and there it is; but I promised no horses, neither shall you have them.' It is perhaps not surprising that the marriage only lasted three weeks. Dr Glen died in 1786.

The other figure in Kay's portrait is James Robertson of Kincraigie in Perthshire, popularly known as 'The Daft Highland Laird' because of his eccentric behaviour. As a young man he had joined the Jacobite army of Bonnie Prince Charlie and had been captured after the defeat at Culloden in April 1746. He was fortunate to be spared execution or transportation to the West Indies or the American colonies – the fate of many captured Jacobites. Instead he was imprisoned in the Tolbooth in Edinburgh. It was during his time in prison that the Laird suffered some sort of mental breakdown that resulted in his release from prison. For the next forty years he roamed the streets of Edinburgh as a harmless eccentric. His brother was appointed as his legal guardian to protect his affairs and Robertson was given an allowance which ensured that he was financially secure.

The Laird was always to be seen wearing his tartan bonnet. Robertson had one ambition and that was to be tried as a Jacobite and hanged, drawn and quartered as a traitor to the House of Hanover. He went out of his way to draw attention to himself as a loyal supporter of the Stewart cause. In vain did he toast the health of the exiled Bonnie Prince Charlie; in vain did he sing Jacobite songs in the taverns of Edinburgh. The Laird even interrupted church services if the minister prayed for King George. The authorities though took pity on him. His insanity gave him immunity from arrest. Although frustrated, Robertson was not to be thwarted. He was determined to be imprisoned again. To achieve this he deliber-ately refused to pay his rent. So to his delight, he was once again locked up in the Tolbooth. His debt was quickly paid by his brother and his release was ordered. But Robertson refused to leave his cell, clinging to the hope that he would yet be sentenced to death for treason. The authorities pleaded with him but to no avail. Rather than physically throw him out, an ingenious plan was agreed by which two armed Town Guardsmen entered his cell to inform Robertson that they were to escort him to the High Court where judges were ready to try him. Robertson leapt up, grabbed his bonnet and followed the guardsmen out through the door of the Tolbooth. You can imagine his dismay when his armed escort raced back inside and locked the door leaving the disappointed Robertson in despair.

Robertson seems to have given up his hopes of being condemned as a Jacobite rebel so he turned his hand quite literally to another way of drawing attention to himself. The Laird was a very skilled wood carver and he now began to carve the likenesses of some of his fellow-citizens which he stuck onto the top of his cane. If he did not like the individual in question then the carved image would be very unflattering. Robertson became a familiar figure on the High Street carrying his decorated cane which often displayed a different carved head, sometimes two, every day. 'Wha hae ye up the day, Laird?' was a popular greeting. When John Kay printed his portrait, Robertson immediately retaliated with a carving of him on his cane. When asked the usual question, he replied 'Don't you see, it's the barber.' Robertson died in July 1790.

From his home in the High Street, from the windows of his premises in nearby Parliament Close and on his walks through the streets of Edinburgh, Kay was able to observe some of the giants of Edinburgh's celebrated late-18th-century 'Golden Age'. Professor Joseph Black, Dr James Hutton, Principal William Robertson, the Reverend Alexander Carlyle, Hugo Arnot, Professor Alexander Munro, Professor John Hope, Lord Kames, Lord Monboddo and Henry Dundas, Viscount Melville, were just some of those leading figures whose likenesses Kay has captured for posterity. In some cases, the caricature drawn and engraved by Kay is the only drawn or painted image that has survived. Such is the case for Adam Smith, the famous economist and author of *The Wealth of Nations*, published in 1776. Apart from a paste cameo miniature of Smith by James Tassie now to be seen in the Scottish National Portrait Gallery, the two prints drawn by Kay are the only likenesses that we have of him. Kay's portrait of Smith beside two of his friends, Lord Rockville and Commissioner Brown, would suggest that the economist was not a very tall man. Another portrait of Smith appears on page 108.

Lord Rockville, Adam Smith and Commissioner Brown.

As well as these intellectual and political giants, Kay also captured the likenesses of leading civic figures like Lord Provost Sir James Hunter Blair and Sir William Forbes of Pitsligo; members of the judiciary like the eccentric Lord Gardenstone and the fearsome Lord Braxfield; national figures residing in Edinburgh like Sir John Sinclair; local celebrities including the notorious Deacon William Brodie and Peter Williamson ('the man from another world' is how he described himself); interesting visitors to Edinburgh like Francis Grose, friend of Robert Burns; and some of the fascinating characters to be found on the Royal Mile such as the Town Crier (see Plate 9), Sedan chairmen (see page 123), fishwives (see page 50), the Town Guard and the 'Sooty Men' (or 'Tron Men'; see page 124) – the chimney sweeps who traditionally walked in front of prisoners condemned to death.

CHAPTER 8

Some Legal Portraits

One of Kay's best-known portraits shows Henry Home (Lord Kames), Hugo Arnot and Lord Monboddo, three of the leading legal figures of their day. Interestingly the portrait is dated 1784. Lord Kames had died in 1782 so Kay must have either used an earlier sketch of Lord Kames or drawn the three characters before the death of Kames and only completed the engraving in 1784.

Henry Home, who was raised to the Scottish bench as Lord Kames in 1752, was a great friend of the historian and philosopher David Hume. Lord Kames, like several of his contemporaries was a very

Lord Kames, Hugo Arnot and Lord Monboddo.

learned man who wrote on several subjects including Scottish history, anthropology and sociology. He was also a leading agricultural improver, who set up a major reclamation project in the Carse of Stirling. He was one of the Scottish judges in the famous case of Joseph Knight who had been enslaved as a young man in Africa. He had survived the fearful passage in a slave ship across the Atlantic to Jamaica. There he had been bought by a Scottish plantation owner, John Wedderburn, whose father had been executed as a Jacobite rebel after Culloden. On his return to Scotland in 1769, Wedderburn brought his slave with him. Knight, however, challenged the legality of his position, arguing that Scots law did not recognise slavery. The judges, including Lord Kames, agreed with Knight declaring that slavery had no place in Scotland. Wedderburn appealed the judgement twice. However, the original decision was upheld and an important legal principle had been established.

The tall thin man in the middle of the portrait is Hugo Arnot of Balcormo. Arnot was a Scottish lawyer, writer and social campaigner. He was the son of a merchant at Leith, the port of Edinburgh, where he was born on 8 December 1749. He changed his name from Pollock to Arnot on succeeding to his mother's property of Balcormo in Fife. He became an advocate in December 1772 which allowed him to plead in court. Arnot soon earned a reputation for his courtroom pleas in defence of his clients. However, Arnot was very much a man of principle. He lost a lot of business by refusing to defend an accused if he thought that they were guilty of the offence for which they had been charged.

Arnot was also a talented writer. In 1779 he published his *History of Edinburgh*. This is an exceptional book as it can be considered as the first seriously researched history of the capital. Arnot drew on a wide range of historical sources including the burgh's own records and the records of the Scottish Parliament. His project seems to have met with considerable help and encouragement from those he consulted. As Arnot records in his Preface:

> I have had to search into most of the publick [sic] records in Scotland. Whether the materials I have discovered be equal to the labour of my researches, is not for me to determine . . . It has afforded me great satisfaction in the

Register House, Edinburgh, from Arnot's *History of Edinburgh*, 2nd edition, 1788.

course of this work, that I have received, on all hands, the most cheerful and liberal assistance. The Town Council of Edinburgh and keepers of all the public records, have given me the most ready access to their repositories.

A second edition was published in 1788, after Arnot's death. This edition was enhanced by twenty beautiful engravings of Edinburgh including the one above of the recently completed Register House at the east end of Princes Street.

In addition, Arnot included an appendix in which he made some fascinating comparisons between the Edinburgh of 1763 and 1783. Arnot clearly was concerned that in this comparatively short period of time there had been a discernible drop in standards of behaviour.

In 1763 a young man was termed 'a fine fellow', who to a well-informed and accomplished mind, added elegance of manners and a conduct guided by principle; one who would not have injured the rights of the meanest individual; who contracted no debts that he could not pay and thought every breach of morality unbecoming the character of a gentleman.

In 1783 the term 'fine fellow' is applied to one who can drink three bottles; who discharges all debts of 'honour' (or game debts and tavern bills), and evades payment of every other; who swears immoderately, and before ladies and talks of his word of honour; who ridicules religion and morality as folly and hypocrisy but without argument; who is very jolly at the table of his friend, and will lose no opportunity of seducing his wife if she is handsome or of debauching his daughter; but, on the mention of such a thing being attempted to his own connections, swears he would cut the throat or blow out the brains of his dearest companion, who would offer such an insult. Sensible mothers should be careful what kind of 'fine fellows' are admitted to visit their families.

In 1785, Arnot also published *A Collection of Celebrated Criminal Trials in Scotland.* This was published at his own expense in defiance of the Edinburgh booksellers. Arnot was concerned at what he perceived to be the harshness of the law and the frequent cases of injustice.

We do not think it possible, that a nation can attain to improvement in science, to refinement of taste, and in manners, without, at the same time, acquiring a refinement in their ideas of justice, and feelings of humanity. The codes of the criminal laws of most nations (our own in no ways excepted) are exceedingly barbarous.

Arnot wrote many papers on local politics. He championed local causes including the proposed imposition of road tolls as a means for funding road projects, which would hurt the poorer citizens. He is said to have delayed for ten years the construction of the city's

South Bridge, completed in 1789, because of the destruction that this project would cause to many householders.

Arnot suffered badly from chronic asthma which was to cause his early death in 1786. His ill-health perhaps contributed to his irritability and occasional rudeness. Many anecdotes are told of his eccentricity. He was one of the first Edinburgh citizens to take up residence in the houses being built in the New Town. His habit of ringing a bell loudly to summon his servant upset one of his new neighbours, an elderly lady. She politely requested that he should stop ringing the bell. Reluctantly Arnot agreed. You can then imagine the shock for his neighbour when, early the next morning, she heard the sound of a pistol being fired in his house. Accompanied by her own servant she rushed next door to find Arnot, dressed in his shirtsleeves, sitting in his armchair holding a smoking pistol. In answer to her question as to what on earth he was doing, he replied that as he could no longer ring his bell, then how else could he summon his servant to shave him in the morning?

By the autumn of 1786, Arnot felt that his end was near. He instructed masons to prepare a suitable enclosure and stone for his impending burial in South Leith Parish Kirkyard. He visited regularly to check on their progress, fearful that he would be dead before they had finished. Thankfully the masons completed their work before his death. Arnot died on 20 November 1786 leaving eight children.

The third character in the portrait on page 84 is James Burnett, Lord Monboddo, who was born in Monboddo House, Kincardinshire, in 1719. Like several of his contemporaries he extended his academic education and was educated at Aberdeen, Edinburgh and Groningen Universities. He earned a reputation as a competent judge who took great care in delivering his opinions but not from the bench. In those days, High Court trials were conducted before a bench of five judges. Monboddo, however, refused to sit beside his colleagues, preferring to sit in the body of the court beside the clerks. This was on account of a judgement in a personal case having gone against him when he had pleaded his own cause.

Like Lord Kames, Monboddo pursued a wide range of interests

OPPOSITE. Lord Monboddo and James Hutton.

beyond the law. He was particularly interested in the origins of language and published his *Origins and Progress of Language* in 1773. That same year he entertained Dr Samuel Johnson, who, accompanied by James Boswell, visited Monboddo House on the way to their famous tour of the Western Isles.

Monboddo was a pioneer anthropologist who was convinced that man was indeed descended from the apes and that there was a midwives' conspiracy: he believed that they cut off the tails of newly born babies. This made Monboddo something of a celebrity. People made a point of walking behind him to see if they could spot his tail. Kay drew two further portraits of Monboddo that made fun of his claims. On page 89 Monboddo on the left is talking to James Hutton with a tiny figure beneath with a tail.

Lord Monboddo's beautiful daughter, Elizabeth, enchanted Robert Burns but tragically she died of consumption at the age of twenty-five at Braid Farm in 1790. In 1791 Burns, who had fallen in love with Elizabeth, wrote a moving poem to her memory.

Elegy on the Late Miss Burnet of Monboddo

Life ne'er exulted in so rich a prize,
As Burnet, lovely from her native skies;
Nor envious death so triumph'd in a blow,
As that which laid th' accomplish'd Burnet low.

Monboddo lived for several years in St John's Street off the Canongate. His home was renowned for the 'learned suppers' he organised at which the table was strewn with roses. Lord Monboddo died in Edinburgh in 1799.

Francis Garden, another key legal figure, was born in Banffshire in 1721. He studied at Aberdeen and Edinburgh and was admitted to the Faculty of Advocates in 1744. He was in Edinburgh in September 1745 and was one of those who joined the Edinburgh Volunteers. He escaped over the town wall before the city was captured by the Jacobites. With some friends, Garden made his way eastwards to link up with the forces of General Cope who had landed at Dunbar on the previous day. Cope was anxious to know what the Jacobites were planning to do. He decided to march his army towards

Francis Garden, Lord Gardenstone.

Edinburgh but was fearful of a surprise attack. Garden and a friend volunteered to go ahead of the army to reconnoitre the Jacobite advance. It was a particularly hot morning so the two men stopped off at a favourite haunt in Musselburgh and amused themselves with sherry and oysters. There they were arrested by an advance party of Highlanders. They could have been shot as spies but were spared because they were so drunk.

Like many of his contemporaries, Garden, now Lord Gardenstone, was a very heavy drinker. His lifestyle was later described in *Kay's Portraits:*

> He was one of those ancient heroes of the bar, who after a night of hard drinking, without having been to bed, and without having studied their causes, would plead with great eloquence upon the mere strength of what they had picked up from the oratory of the opposite counsel.

Judges and senior law officers were particularly prone to over-indulgence. This was due in part to the practice in the High Court of cases continuing until a verdict was reached.

St Bernard's Well on the Water of Leith.

This often meant, as we shall see in the cases of Deacon William Brodie and Thomas Muir, that trials could last right through the night and into the following day. Judges took to refreshing themselves at the bench with glasses of wine or brandy taken with dry biscuits.

Francis Garden was raised to the bench in 1764 as Lord Gardenstone. He took up residence in Morningside House, then a little country village to the south of Edinburgh, and rode into the Courts each day on a horse. Kay's portrait shows Gardenstone sitting rather uncomfortably on his steed as he was far from being a confident rider. He is followed by his little servant boy whom he insisted on dressing in a kilt. Gardenstone was taking advantage of the recent ending of the Dress Act of 1746 which had outlawed the wearing of tartan and which had only been repealed in 1782. In addition to his duties on the Bench, Lord Gardenstone improved his estates in Angus and built the model village of Laurencekirk. Like several of his land-owning contemporaries, Gardenstone was a great supporter of agricultural improvement. At the time of his death the village of Laurencekirk contained five hundred houses. To encourage the growth of the village, he offered land on very easy terms, and built an inn. He also founded a library, a school and a museum for the use of the villagers, and did his best to establish spinning and weaving in the village.

In 1788, Gardenstone paid for the construction of the charming St Bernard's Well by the Water of Leith. The Well was designed by the celebrated Edinburgh landscape painter Alexander Nasmyth who modelled the Well on the Temple of Vesta at Tivoli in Italy. At the centre of an open pillared dome stands a marble statue of Hygieia, Goddess of Health.

Gardenstone was a noted eccentric. He was often seen walking in the High Street accompanied by his pet pig which he took to bed with him each night as a bed-warmer. He claimed that his little pig kept its heat throughout the night unlike a warming pan. Robert Chambers relates that when the pig was too big to get into bed, Gardenstone would make a bed for his pet in front of the fire and wrap his clothes around it so that they were warm in the morning. One late-night visitor described how he had tripped over the sleeping pig in the gloom. Lord Gardenstone died at his home in Morningside in 1793.

Undoubtedly the most formidable and feared judge on the Scottish bench in the later years of the 18th century was Robert McQueen, Lord Braxfield. Robert McQueen was born in Lanarkshire in 1722. His father was a lawyer and became Sheriff-Substitute for the Upper Ward of Lanark. He was educated at Lanark Grammar School followed by Edinburgh University where he studied law. He was apprenticed to Thomas Goudie with a view to becoming a Writer to the Signet (a private society of Scottish solicitors). He was given the responsibility of managing his employer's cases that were being tried in the Court of Session where civil cases were heard. McQueen was fascinated by the nature of Court work and determined to become an advocate – a practising Court lawyer.

Braxfield devoted himself to a study of civil and feudal law. He became a member of the Faculty of Advocates in 1746 and was extremely fortunate to be appointed as Council for the Crown in dealing with issues relating to the Forfeited Estates (Estates forfeited by the Government from clan chiefs who had supported the

Robert McQueen, Lord Braxfield.

Jacobite cause in 1745/1746), where his knowledge of feudal law stood him in good stead.

Like many of his contemporaries he was in the habit of taking briefings in a tavern and like them he was renowned for his heavy drinking. He would often hear cases with a bottle of claret, a glass and a plate of biscuits on the bench in front of him. He shone at Court work and was known to present sometimes as many as fifteen, even twenty, cases in one day. McQueen was called to the Bench in 1766, taking the title of Lord Braxfield. He was described as being 'hard headed, hard-hearted and hard drinking'. He was famous for his earthy comments from the Bench. One such being 'Gin ye hang a thief when he's young, you'll nae hang him when he's auld.' And when two counsel appeared before him obviously suffering from a hard night's drinking:

> Gentlemen, ye may just pack up your papers and gang hame.
> The tane o' ye's rifting punch and the ither's belching claret
> – and there'll be nae gude got out o' ye the day.

His blunt use of the Scots tongue and coarseness were both legendary. After his first wife died leaving him with four young children to bring up, Braxfield wasted no time in courting Elizabeth Ord, daughter of Lord Chief Justice, Baron Ord. One morning Braxfield approached the young lady near his home in George Square. 'Lizzy, I am looking out fer a wife and I thocht you just the person that would suit me. Let me ha'e yer answer aff or on, the morn and nae mair aboot it.' The young lady accepted this rather brusque proposal.

His further advancement was helped by his connections with the powerful Dundas family. Lord President Dundas was a near-neighbour and his brother, Henry Dundas, was soon to be Viscount Melville, 'the uncrowned king of Scotland'.

Braxfield was appointed Lord Justice Clerk, Scotland's senior judge, in 1788. As Lord Justice, Braxfield presided over the notorious political trials of the 1790s, including the trial of Thomas Muir. (See chapter 15.)

Writing in 1837, Hugh Paton, the publisher of *Kay's Portraits*, reflected the very mixed feelings generated by Lord Braxfield's conduct as senior trial judge.

> During the eventful period Lord Braxfield displayed what he conceived to be his duty with firmness and in accordance to the letter and spirit of the law if not always with the leniency and moderation which in the present day would have been deemed essential . . . The conduct of Lord Braxfield during these memorable trials has indeed been freely censured in recent times as having been distinguished by great and unnecessary severity. But the truth is he was extremely well-fitted for the crisis . . . for by the bold and

fearless front he assumed at a time when every other person in authority quailed beneath the gathering storm, he contributed not a little to curb the lawless spirit that was abroad and which threatened a repetition of that reign of terror and anarchy which so fearfully devastated a neighbouring country [France].

However, in his memoirs, Henry, Lord Cockburn, was severely critical of Braxfield's conduct on the bench:

> But the giant of the bench was Braxfield. His very name makes people start yet [1856]. Strong built and dark, with rough eyebrows, powerful eyes, threatening lips and a low, growling voice, he was like a formidable blacksmith . . . His accent and his dialect were exaggerated Scotch; his language like his thoughts, short, strong and conclusive . . . Illiterate and without any taste for refined enjoyment [or] strength of understanding, which gave him power without cultivation, only encouraged him to a more contemptuous disdain of all natures less coarse than his own . . . A dexterous and practical trier of ordinary cases, he was harsh to prisoners even in his jocularity, and to every counsel who he chose to dislike . . . It may be doubted if he was ever so much in his element as when tauntingly repelling the last despairing claim of a wretched culprit and sending him to Botany Bay or the gallows with an insulting jest; over which he would chuckle the more when observing that correct people were shocked. It is impossible to condemn his conduct as a criminal judge too gravely or too severely. It was a disgrace to the age.

Influential contemporaries in the legal profession were indeed shocked by his conduct which they felt had discredited Scottish justice. Perhaps surprisingly given his reputation, Braxfield was a supporter of the work of Robert Owen, the philanthropist and social reformer, at New Lanark, and Braxfield Row in the model village is named after him. Braxfield was the inspiration for the character of Lord Weir in Robert Louis Stevenson's unfinished novel *Weir of Hermiston*. He died at his home in Edinburgh's George Square in 1799.

CHAPTER 9

Some Civic Portraits

James Hunter was born in Ayr in 1740 and educated at the local school. He came to Edinburgh and took up a position with Coutts Bank, rising to become the bank's director. He married well and took the surname of Blair in recognition of the estate that he inherited in Ayrshire.

Blair set about improving his new inheritance. He built a new harbour at Portpatrick and introduced a packet ferry to Ireland. Blair encouraged agricultural improvement throughout the county of Ayrshire. He had a reputation for being an excellent businessman. He was elected as Edinburgh's MP in 1781 but resigned his seat, preferring to take on the role of Lord Provost in 1784. Blair campaigned vigorously for improvements to the Old Town, particularly access to the spreading suburbs of the south. Against much opposition, led by Hugo Arnot, he pushed through proposals for the construction of the South Bridge.

Edinburgh University had been founded in 1582 and was known as 'The Toun's College'. It was located to the south of the Old Town outside the burgh walls on the site of the Kirk o' Field where Henry Darnley, husband of Mary, Queen of Scots, had been murdered in February 1567. The accommodation was no longer fit for purpose, particularly with a steep rise in the number of undergraduates which by 1789 was approaching 1,000.

Blair pushed through plans to provide new accommodation and the famous architect Robert Adam was commissioned to draw up plans for the project. The foundation stone of what is still known

Sir James Hunter Blair.

as 'The Old Quad' was laid in 1789 by Lord Napier, the Grand
Master Mason of Scotland (see Plate 10). Blair died in 1787, however,
so never saw his project completed. Blair Street and Hunter Square,
to the south of the High Street, were named in his honour.

Sir William Forbes of Pitsligo was born in Edinburgh in 1739. His
family background was particularly interesting as on his mother's
side he was related to Lord Pitsligo, a determined Jacobite. Lord
Pitsligo had 'come out' (fought as a Jacobite) in both 1715 and, at
the age of sixty-seven, in 1745. He survived the Battle of Culloden

but he was now a fugitive with a price on his head and the prospect of execution as a traitor to the House of Hanover. Lord Pitsligo was hidden by his people for safety until his death in 1762. He spent much of his time in a cave on his estate but on one occasion he was nearly captured in the house of a kinswoman. He was hidden in a cupboard behind the bed occupied by an old lady. The searching soldiers apologised to her for their intrusion.

William Forbes' father died when he was only four so his mother turned to her Pitsligo relatives for help. He was brought to Edinburgh in 1753 aged fourteen and with the help of these relations obtained a position in the banking house of Messrs Coutts working as a clerk. After serving a seven-year apprenticeship he was offered a partnership in the bank and in 1763 he formed a new company with Sir William Forbes, Sir Robert Herries and Sir James Hunter-Blair, the future Lord Provost.

As well as being a very successful banker, Forbes was renowned for his charitable works. He became a manager of both the Charity Workhouse and the Orphans' Hospital. Sir William also became a manager of the Royal Infirmary, the Blind Asylum and the Lunatic Asylum. He was an active supporter of the construction of a new building for Edinburgh's High School, opened in 1777. (This building, now part of Edinburgh University, still stands at the foot of Infirmary Street.)

Sir William was considered by his contemporaries as:

A man full of practical knowledge and enlightened benevolence ... In short no improvements were contemplated, and no benevolent work projected, which did not find in Sir William ready and efficient support.

In 1781 he succeeded as heir to the Barony of Pitsligo. He purchased an additional seventy acres of adjoining land and set about its improvement. He had new cottages built for his tenants, encouraged improved methods of farming and built the model village of New Pitsligo. There he established a bleach field for linen and started a spinning school for local women and girls. He also opened a school for the children of his tenants. Sir William was a devoted member of the Scottish Episcopalian Church and funded several new church buildings. This part of his charitable good work was

THE GOOD SHALL MOURN A BROTHER — ALL A FRIEND

ABOVE. The High School building on Infirmary Street, founded 1777.

OPPOSITE. Sir William Forbes of Pitsligo. In the background Kay shows
Sir William giving money to two poor people.

carried on by two of his sons after his death. His eldest son Sir
William helped fund the construction of St John's at the West End
of Princes Street while his second son, Lord Medwyn, helped fund
St Paul's in York Place. In 1784, Sir William was admitted to the
Merchant Company of Edinburgh, becoming Master in 1786, a
position he held again in 1802. During his term of office he did
much to promote the charitable work of the Company in their
support of widows and their children and contributed to the
drawing up of new legislation dealing with bankruptcy.

Sir William was very much a part of Edinburgh's 'Golden Age'.
He was a founder member of the Antiquarian Society and entered
into correspondence with many of the leading men of his day.
Amongst his friends was the artist Sir Joshua Reynolds, whom he
had met on his business trips to London. Sir Joshua painted Sir
William twice. Sir William also befriended some of the leading
political figures of his day including Henry Dundas, Viscount
Melville, the 'uncrowned king of Scotland', who controlled Scotland
for the Prime Minister, William Pitt, in the 1790s. Sir William was a
very modest and unambitious man. He was offered and turned

down the parliamentary seats of Edinburgh and Aberdeenshire as well as a peerage by Pitt.

Sir William's health declined in the 1790s but he continued to support his wide range of good causes. In 1806 Sir William was summoned to London to appear as a character witness at the trial of Viscount Melville accused of misappropriating Navy funds. His testimony helped in the acquittal of Melville but the effort proved too much for him. Sir William was brought back to Edinburgh very ill and died surrounded by family and friends on 12 November 1806.

Kay's portrait of Sir William is interesting as it looks as though he has been sketched posing at the window of his office overlooking Parliament Close. (He was in fact a near neighbour of Kay's.) Kay often added a personal comment at the foot of his portraits. Sometimes these were factual; sometimes they were amusing; sometimes they reflected very much Kay's personal opinions. In the case of Sir William, Kay clearly expressed the feelings of many of his fellow-citizens when he added the following comment at the foot of Sir William's portrait: 'The good shall mourn a brother – all a friend.'

Sir John Sinclair was born in Thurso Castle, Caithness, in 1756. He studied Law at Glasgow, Edinburgh and Oxford Universities and was admitted to both the Scottish and English Bars. He had a passionate interest in improving agriculture in Scotland. He was the first to introduce Cheviot sheep to the Highlands and, in 1793, founded the Scottish Board of Agriculture to promote agricultural improvement. In 1784 he published his *History of the Revenue of the British Empire*. His many talents were recognised and he was a Fellow of both the Royal Society of London and that of Edinburgh.

Amongst his many achievements was the creation of *The First Statistical Account of Scotland*, which was published by the Edinburgh publisher William Creech, in which the word 'statistics' was used for the first time. This was a most ambitious enterprise. Sinclair, at his own expense, wrote to every Church of Scotland parish minister (more than 900!) and asked them to reply to a series of questions about their parish. In all he listed 160 questions for the ministers to answer. He was interested to know about such things as location, population, agriculture, industry, education, climate,

OPPOSITE. Sir John Sinclair.

The Scottish Patriot.

significant changes since 1760, any events of note and so on. The returns from the parish ministers were published as they arrived back to Sir John who was helped in this most ambitious project by the publisher William Smellie. In all twenty-one volumes were produced between 1791 and 1799. Some ministers provided Sir John with very full answers to his questions. Others were not nearly so thorough. William Creech was so disappointed with the Edinburgh returns that he added his own analysis for Sir John. The *Statistical Account* gives a unique insight into life in Scotland at the end of the 18th century, and was the first project of its type in the world.

Sir John served for many years as an MP and was a member of the Privy Council. He was a financial adviser to Prime Minister William Pitt during the French Revolutionary War. He died in 1835.

Sir John had a very large family and had to move from his beautiful house in the recently-completed Charlotte Square in Edinburgh's New Town to a bigger house round the corner in George Street. He had two children by his first wife and thirteen by his second! Like their father, the children were all very tall, either just below or over six feet. It must have been quite a sight to see them on their way out together. Their neighbours joked that the pavement in front of their house in George Street should be renamed 'The Giants' Causeway'.

Just a few metres down the High Street from where John Kay lived, a plaque marks the site of the shop of James Gillespie.

James Gillespie of Spylaw, working in partnership with his brother John, had a well-known tobacconist and snuff shop here. The brothers were typically canny Scots businessmen who gradually amassed a small fortune from their endeavours. Their business was one of the first to trade with the newly-independent United States of America.

In 1759 they purchased the snuff mills in Colinton that were powered by the Water of Leith. The plaque is perhaps mistaken in that in *Kay's Portraits* it is stated that it was James Gillespie who oversaw the manufacturing side of the business while it was John who managed the shop. However, Peter Williamson's Edinburgh Street Directory for June 1786 to June 1788 includes: 'James Gillespie,

OPPOSITE. The plaque of James Gillespie's shop.

FORMERLY
THE SHOP OF
JAMES GILLESPIE
OF SPYLAW
TOBACCO AND SNUFF
MANUFACTURER
FOUNDER OF
JAMES GILLESPIE'S
HOSPITAL
AND SCHOOLS
DIED 8 APRIL 1797

ERECTED BY
THE GOVERNORS 1885

James and John Gillespie.

Tobacconist opposite the Guard' (the Guard House located in the High Street).

The brothers purchased the estates of Spylaw, Bonaly and Fernielaw which were close to their mill. In 1773 they built Spylaw House on the site of an older property.

The brothers never married and lived very frugally. The one luxury that they allowed themselves was the purchase of a bright yellow coach. Passers-by on the High Street were astonished one morning to see this luxurious coach come clattering up and stopping outside the brothers' shop. This prompted one eye-witness Henry Erskine, the witty Lord Advocate, realising where the brothers had made their money, to remark:

> Wha wad hae thocht it
> That noses could hae bocht it!

Shrewd investments in tobacco plantations added to their wealth. John died in 1795 followed by James in 1797. He divided his fortune between two charitable Edinburgh enterprises – a hospital for needy senior citizens and a school for poor children, now James Gillespie's High School.

CHAPTER 10

Some Portraits of the 'Golden Age'

Today it is from Scotland that we get rules of taste in all the arts from epic poetry to gardening.

(Voltaire 1762)

More true learning is to be found in Edinburgh than in Oxford and Cambridge taken together.

(J.W. von Archenholz 1780)

Taken altogether I do not know any other town where it would be pleasanter to live. [Edinburgh] is in a great degree the Geneva of Britain.

(Louis Simond 1815)

Clearly in the eyes of contemporaries, Edinburgh had acquired a considerable reputation as a centre of learning and culture. The second half of the 18th century saw an intellectual flowering in Edinburgh which has come to be described as the 'Golden Age'. A combination of factors, not least the growing reputation of Edinburgh University, saw a gathering in Edinburgh of a group of remarkable men. Interestingly very few of this group were actually Edinburgh-born. Most had moved to Edinburgh to further their careers and to enjoy the company of their peers. They met socially and debated topical issues in organisations such as the Select Society, the Philosophical Society and the Society of Antiquaries. Here academics were joined by leading civic figures such as the

The Author of the Wealth of Nations

Reverend Alexander Carlyle who we met first in chapter 2 and Henry Erskine, the eloquent Lord Advocate.

The father-figure was undoubtedly David Hume but he had died in 1776 so Kay did not get the opportunity to draw his portrait. However, there are portraits of such leading figures as Adam Smith, Professor Joseph Black and James Hutton.

Adam Smith was born in Kirkcaldy in 1723. He moved to Edinburgh in 1748. In 1751, Smith was appointed firstly to the Chair of Logic at Glasgow University and later to the Chair of Moral Philosophy. He then took up the position of Tutor to the 3rd Duke of Buccleuch and accompanied him to France where, like David Hume, he met many of the leading intellectual lights. Adam Smith moved to London and there in 1776 he had published *Inquiry into the Nature and Causes of the Wealth of Nations*. This book introduced the concepts of the division of labour, the function of market forces and, of course, the idea of free trade. The book was an instant success. He returned to Edinburgh that same year and took up residence in Panmure House in the Canongate. Smith witnessed the death of his friend Hume in his New Town home. Smith was Hume's executor and organised the publication of Hume's papers. In 1778 Smith was appointed as the Commissioner of Customs in Edinburgh. He was appointed as the Lord Rector of Glasgow University in 1787. Smith died in 1790.

Kay drew two portraits of Smith. The one shown here certainly looks as though it is posed with Smith perhaps being drawn in his study. The only other known contemporary image of Smith is a Tassie medallion made in 1787, now on display in the Scottish National Portrait Gallery in Edinburgh.

Joseph Black was born in Bordeaux in 1728. He was the son of a Scottish wine merchant. He was appointed in 1766 as Professor of Medicine and of Chemistry at Edinburgh University. Black is best known for his theory of latent heat. Black first demonstrated the qualities of 'fixed air' (carbon dioxide). Kay's portrait shows Black in typical lecturing pose. The empty cage on the left and the dead bird on the bench suggest that he has been demonstrating the gas.

OPPOSITE. Adam Smith.

Joseph Black.

There was very much a practical side to his research. His work
encouraged advances in several industrial processes including the
application of lime in bleaching; the extraction of alkali from kelp
and improvements to pottery glazing. His research on evaporation
and latent heat contributed to the work of the Scottish engineer
James Watt at Glasgow University. At a supper party in 1770 he
amazed his guests by demonstrating a hydrogen balloon which he
released and, as if by magic, the astonished guests saw the balloon
floating to the ceiling. Professor Black died in 1799.

Joseph Black's great friend was his fellow-bachelor James Hutton,
considered by many to be the 'Father of Modern Geology'. James

Hutton was born in Edinburgh in 1726 and attended the local High School. After three years studying at Edinburgh University, he went to the University of Paris to continue his studies, taking the degree of Doctor of Medicine at Leiden University in 1749 with a thesis on blood circulation.

Hutton returned to Edinburgh and did some experimental work in the production of dyes and for a short while ran a business with a partner manufacturing crystalline salt required for metalworking and dyeing. In the 1750s Hutton left Edinburgh and took over the running of two farms in Berwickshire that he had inherited from his father. He set about introducing improvements, including upgrading the drainage of the fields. It was while engaged in this work that Hutton developed his fascination for the composition and appearance of the stones unearthed. Hutton also took a keen interest in the rock formations that he observed on the Berwickshire coast.

In 1764, he went on a geological tour of the north-west of Scotland with his friend George Maxwell-Clerk. In 1770 Hutton returned to Edinburgh to a house at St John's Hill overlooking the Salisbury Crags in the shadow of Arthur's Seat, an extinct volcano. Here he carried out valuable field work where he observed clear evidence of the intrusion of molten volcanic rock into the older sedimentary rocks. It was clear to Hutton that the geological age of the Earth had to be significantly older than the accepted biblical age.

Hutton worked on his theory for some twenty-five years. At last he felt ready to share his findings with friends and colleagues. However, he was acutely conscious that his ideas would be seen as very controversial and indeed heretical. Hutton was by nature a very nervous man so it was on 7 March 1785 that his friend Professor Joseph Black read the first part of his paper outlining his theories on the geology of the earth to the Royal Society of Edinburgh. The paper was very well received so Hutton himself read the second part at the next meeting on 4 April. His thesis was that the Earth had a molten core; that the Earth's surface had undergone immense change; that the Earth was experiencing 'constant destruction and renewal' and that the Earth was therefore not as originally created and had 'no vestige of a beginning; no prospect of an end'. Hutton followed this up with a series of fieldwork expeditions to various parts of Scotland. In 1795 he published his findings in his *Theory of the Earth; with Proofs and Illustrations*. Hutton was a true giant of

the Golden Age, who blew apart the worlds of science and religion.

In his notes, Kay describes an amusing anecdote about Joseph Black and James Hutton – both bachelors and good friends. Kay records how several literary figures in Edinburgh decided to hold a 'convivial meeting' once a week. They decided to call themselves 'The Oyster Club', oysters being their favourite dish which they would eat while they discussed topical issues. The two friends were deputed to find suitable premises. They found what looked like the ideal venue on the recently constructed South Bridge advertised as 'Stewart, Vintner, downstairs'. They found the room very much to their liking and so meetings were arranged for the club. The group met for most of that winter but one evening Dr Hutton arrived late for the meeting. As Kay records:

> Dr Hutton being rather late, was surprised, when going in, to see a whole bevy of well-dressed but somewhat brazen-faced young ladies brush past him, and take refuge in an adjoining apartment. He then for the first time, began to think that all was not right, and communicated his suspicions to the rest of the company. Next morning the notable discovery was made, that our amiable philosophers had introduced their friends to one of the most noted houses of bad fame in the city!!

James Hutton died in 1797 and was buried in the Greyfriars Kirkyard. Two years later, his friend Joseph Black was laid to rest beside him.

Another giant of the 'Golden Age' was the Reverend William Robertson, who was to become the Principal of Edinburgh University. Robertson was born in 1721 in Borthwick, Midlothian. He studied divinity in Edinburgh and in 1743 was ordained Minister of Gladsmuir Parish in his native county. In 1756 he moved to Lady Yester's Parish in Edinburgh. Robertson now took up a serious interest in History and in 1759 wrote a very popular *History of*

OPPOSITE. In this portrait Kay shows James Hutton, with his geological hammer, tackling the solid mass of the establishment, whose profiles would have been recognisable at the time.

PHILOSOPHERS

ABOVE. James Hutton and Joseph Black.

OPPOSITE. William Robertson, Principal of Edinburgh University.

Scotland focusing particularly on the reign of Mary, Queen of Scots. This was very much a ground-breaking book as Robertson sought out original source material, travelling as far as London and Oxford to support his arguments.

In 1761, Robertson was appointed as joint Minister of Greyfriars Church and Royal Chaplain. In 1762 he was appointed as Principal of Edinburgh University and so was the academic leader for much of the 'Golden Age'. Other works include *History of Charles V* (1769) and the *History of America* (1772). Robertson died in 1792.

Professor John Hope was born in born in Edinburgh in 1725. He was the son of surgeon Robert Hope and Marion Glas. Hope studied medicine at Edinburgh University. Like several of his contemporaries, he continued his education on the Continent studying botany in Paris. Hope returned to his studies in Scotland, graduating MD from the University of Glasgow in 1750. Hope moved back to Edinburgh and for the next decade he practised medicine, indulging in botany in his spare time. In 1760, Hope was

KAY. fect 1790

His Majestys Historiographer

appointed as King's Botanist and as Professor of Botany at Edinburgh University.

Kay's charming portrait of John Hope (the only image that we have of him) shows him greeting one of his gardeners, and will be familiar to visitors to Edinburgh's Royal Botanic Garden. The Garden's new entrance, the John Hope Gateway, opened in 2009 and is named in his honour.

In 1763, Hope succeeding in combining the gardens and collections at Trinity Hospital and Holyrood to a new, combined site on the road to Leith. He also succeeded in obtaining a permanent endowment for the garden, thus establishing arguably the first ever 'Royal Botanic Garden'. He was elected a Fellow of the Royal Society in February 1767 and served as President of the Royal College of Physicians of Edinburgh, 1784–6. Hope died in 1786.

Our last two characters, Andrew Bell and William Smellie, would doubtless have been amused to find themselves grouped with some of the leading lights of Edinburgh's 'Golden Age'. Nevertheless their work together certainly enhanced Edinburgh's growing reputation as a centre of learning.

William Smellie was born in Edinburgh in 1740. After completing his apprenticeship, Smellie opened his printing business in Anchor Close, just east of the City Chambers in the High Street, and so was a very near-neighbour of John Kay. Smellie was a very successful businessman and was to become Edinburgh's best-known printer and publisher of the day. In 1768, in collaboration with Andrew Bell and Colin MacFarquhar, Smellie published the first edition of *The Encyclopaedia Britannica*. Smellie wrote most of the articles for the ambitious project. Smellie is also remembered for other notable publishing projects. He helped Sir John Sinclair with the mammoth task of editing and publishing *The Statistical Account of Scotland* (1791–9) which, as noted on page 102, gives an invaluable insight into the Scotland of the 1790s.

Smellie was a friend of the poet Robert Burns who described him as 'that old veteran of genius, wit and bawdy'. The two men were frequent drinking companions and Smellie introduced Burns to

OPPOSITE. Professor John Hope greeting a gardener in Edinburgh's Royal Botanic Garden.

ABOVE. Andrew Bell and William Smellie.

OPPOSITE. The title page of the first collected edition of the articles written for
The Encyclopaedia Britannica published in 1771.

several of Edinburgh's well-known clubs, including the Crochallan
Fencibles which met in Anchor Close, very near to Kay's home in
the High Street. Smellie printed the Edinburgh Edition of Burns'
poems for the publisher William Creech in 1787. Smellie continued
to publish a wide variety of works, including his two-volume *Philosophy of Natural History*, which became a set text at Harvard University in the 19th century. Smellie was also a noted antiquarian and
was a founder member of the Scottish Society of Antiquaries (1780).
He died in 1795. He too is buried in Greyfriars Kirkyard.

Kay's portrait above of Andrew Bell on the left and William Smellie
on the right confirms that Kay drew his characters as he saw them.

Encyclopædia Britannica;

OR, A

D·I·C·T·I·O·N·A·R·Y

OF

ARTS and SCIENCES,

COMPILED UPON A NEW PLAN.

IN WHICH

The different SCIENCES and ARTS are digested into
distinct Treatises or Systems;

AND

The various TECHNICAL TERMS, &c. are explained as they occur
in the order of the Alphabet.

ILLUSTRATED WITH ONE HUNDRED AND SIXTY COPPERPLATES.

By a SOCIETY of GENTLEMEN in SCOTLAND.

IN THREE VOLUMES.

VOL. III.

EDINBURGH:
Printed for A. BELL and C. MACFARQUHAR;
And sold by COLIN MACFARQUHAR, at his Printing-office, Nicolson-street.
M.DCC.LXXI.

As can be seen, Bell had misshaped legs and a very prominent nose! This rather unflattering portrait may explain why so many of Kay's plates were never published as perhaps subjects who took exception to their portraiture by Kay purchased the plate and had it destroyed.

Andrew Bell was born in Edinburgh in 1726. His father was a baker. He had little formal education and was apprenticed to the engraver Richard Cooper. Bell was acutely conscious of the size of his nose. He kept an outsize papier-mâché nose in his pocket. Whenever anyone stared at his natural nose he would slip on the fake nose when they were not looking to shock them. Bell was very short in stature: only 4 foot 6 inches tall. Despite his small stature, Bell deliberately rode the tallest horse available in Edinburgh. He was followed around by a servant-boy carrying a ladder which he would hold while Bell dismounted to the cheers of onlookers.

Bell began work as an engraver of crests, names and addresses on dog collars. He then went into partnership with Colin MacFarquhar, an Edinburgh bookseller, to produce the comprehensive reference work to be known as *The Encyclopaedia Britannica*. The pair approached Smellie to write the articles for the planned encyclopaedia. MacFarquhar would do the editing while Bell would produce the copperplate engravings. Bell set to work and produced one hundred and sixty detailed engravings for the first edition of the work published in 1768. He subsequently produced engravings for the next three editions of the encyclopaedia. The fourth edition was illustrated with five hundred and thirty-one of Bell's engravings.

For the first edition, Bell produced three full pages of anatomically accurate depictions of dissected female pelvises and of foetuses in wombs for the midwifery article. The completed encyclopaedia was presented to King George III in London. However, these illustrations shocked the king, who commanded that the offending pages be ripped from every copy in London. After MacFarquhar died in 1793, Bell bought out his heirs and became sole owner of the *Britannica* until his own death in 1809.

1. Self-portrait, John Kay: a rare example painted in oils.

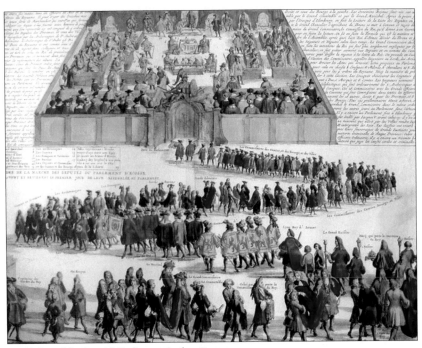

2. A sitting of the Scottish Parliament in the 1680s.

3. The Edinburgh Town Guard in front of the Tolbooth, drawn by John Kay c. 1790.

4. Prince Charles Edward Stuart, 1720–1788 ('Bonnie Prince Charlie'), painted by Allan Ramsay during the occupation of Edinburgh in 1745.

5. Edinburgh Castle in the 18th century.

6. David Hume, 1711–1776, historian and philosopher, painted by Allan Ramsay, son of the poet Allan Ramsay, in 1766.

7. George Drummond (1687–1766), Lord Provost of Edinburgh, painted by Sir George Chalmers.

8. James Craig (1739–1795), architect for Edinburgh's New Town, painted by David Allan.

9. John Kay's drawing of the Town Crier accompanied by a drummer from the Town Guard.

10. The laying of the foundation stone for the Old Quad of Edinburgh University, 1789. (David Allan, 1789). This clearly shows the destruction to property caused by the building of the South Bridge.

11. (*Right*) Portrait of Robert Burns.

12. (*Below*) King George IV's landing at Leith on 15 August 1822 (William Home Lizars).

13. (*Bottom*) Parliament Close from John Kay's workshop window by Sir David Wilkie (depicting a scene from before 1796) with figures based on caricatures by John Kay painted by Alexander Fraser and William Kidd.

CHAPTER 11
Some Local
Portraits

————————

As well as drawing leading celebrities of his day, Kay has left us a series of charming portraits of some of the characters of the streets of Edinburgh. These entertaining illustrations complement the description of Edinburgh written by Robert Chambers and quoted on page 53.

Our first portrait shows the tall, thin lawyer Hugo Arnot giving some money to a man called John Duncan, a street beggar who was known as 'Gingerbread Jock'. John Duncan had fallen on hard times and for many years took up a position in Parliament Close outside John Kay's workshop. Here he would place five pieces of gingerbread on the ground and invite passers-by to knock them over with a thrown stick for which he charged a halfpenny. Any pieces knocked over could be kept. However, there were very few winners as Duncan secured the pieces of gingerbread on the ground in such a manner as it was almost impossible to knock them over.

The illustration on page 123 shows Donald Black and Donald Kennedy, two of Edinburgh's Sedan chairmen. The two men are taking a rest in Parliament Close with the old Scottish Parliament building in the background. Black is offering his fellow chairman a pinch of snuff. Like most of Edinburgh's chairmen, Black and Kennedy were Highlanders. Edinburgh's steep and narrow streets and closes made a carriage and horses impracticable. Sedan chairmen were very much in demand. The Society of Edinburgh

John Duncan and Hugo Arnot.

Chairmen was formed in 1740 and as with today's taxi drivers, the chairmen were licensed and regulated by the burgh council.

Like the Sedan chairmen, the 'Sooty Men' – the burgh's chimney sweeps, or 'Tron Men' (page 124) – were organised into a society and regulated by the council. Their distinctive uniform of flat bonnets, a long coat, a short leather apron, knee breeches and buckled shoes has been accurately captured by Kay. The men are carrying the tools of their trade – a ladder, a broom (or 'besom' in Scots), a coil of ropes and a weighted ball.

The Tron Men also acted as firefighters for the burgh. They were

Sedan chairmen.

lodged in part of the old City Guard House just outside Kay's home
in the High Street.

The squat single-storey Guard House (page 125) sat in the middle
of the High Street. On the left of the picture you can see two Tron
Men setting off on a call with their ladders. The sentry-box at the
front was a favourite target for Edinburgh youths who delighted in
creeping up and tipping it over with the Town Guardsman stuck
inside. To the right of the building what looks like a rocking horse
was instead the Edinburgh equivalent of the stocks. Guardsmen

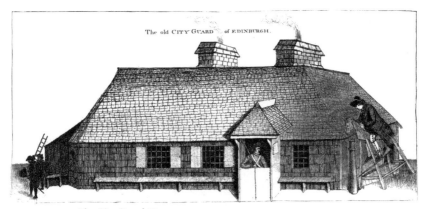

The old CITY GUARD of EDINBURGH.

ABOVE. The City Guard House.

OPPOSITE. The Tron Men: chimney sweeps.

who had breached regulations or locals arrested for drunken behaviour would be placed on the horse and their feet tied to muskets. They would then be exposed to the abuse of their fellow-citizens which could involve having stones, muck and even cats thrown at them. Traditionally the Tron Men walked in front of condemned criminals on their way to execution.

Edinburgh was renowned for its many taverns. One of the favourites was Johnnie Dowie's Tavern located in Libberton's Wynd on the site of the present-day George IV Bridge. Robert Burns was a regular customer on his visits to Edinburgh.

Robert Chambers described Dowie's Tavern thus:

A great portion of this house consisting of a series of windowless chambers, decreasing in size till the last was a mere box, of irregular oblong figure, jocularly, but not inappropriately, designated the Coffin. Beside these there were two rooms possessing light, and as that came from a deep, narrow alley, it was light little more than in name. Hither, nevertheless did many of the Parliament House men [the judges and lawyers] come daily for their merriment. Here, nightly assembled companies of cits [those not considered to be gentlemen] as well as men of wit and of fashion, to spend hours in . . . gentle conviviality. The place is said to

I KAY 1813

A' YE WHA WIS' ON E' ENINGS LANG, TO MEET AN' CRACK AN' SING A SANG,
AN' WEET YOUR PIPES, FOR LITTLE WRANG, TO PURSE OR PERSON
TO SERE.ˢ JOHNNIE DOWIE'S GANG THERE THRUM A VERSE ON.

ABOVE. *A Sleepy Congregation* by John Kay.

OPPOSITE. Johnnie Dowie.

have been a howff of Fergusson [the Edinburgh poet Robert Fergusson] and Burns . . . John Dowie's was chiefly celebrated for its ale – Younger's Edinburgh Ale – a potent fluid which almost glued the lips of the drinker together and of which few therefore could despatch more than a bottle.

Kay was quite prepared to poke fun at his fellow-citizens. In *A Sleepy Congregation* he shows Dr Alexander Webster, minister of the

Tolbooth Kirk, preaching a sermon. The Tolbooth Kirk occupied the
south-west area of St Giles' Kirk which at that time housed four
separate churches. Below Dr Webster is the precentor, John Campbell.
At this time there was still no instrumental music permitted in church
services so the precentor led the congregation in the singing of the
psalms. What is amusing is that Kay has drawn many recognisable
figures in the congregation most of whom are shown to be fast asleep.

John Kay also recorded some contemporary incidents such as the
repaving of the High Street and the fierce argument concerning
what came to be known as 'The Earthen Mound' or 'Geordie Boyd's
Mud Brig'. The original plan of James Craig for the New Town had
assumed that the main link with the Old Town was to be the North
Bridge. Craig had proposed the draining of the Nor' Loch which by
the 1760s was little better than an open sewer. Once drained, there
was to be a canal built in the valley that separated the Old Town
from the New. In 1763 work started on draining the waters of the
Nor' Loch which covered the area now occupied by Princes Street
Gardens and the Waverley Station. In 1765 Lord Provost George
Drummond laid the foundation stone for the North Bridge. This
was his last public act. He died the following year. Unfortunately
poor construction work resulted in part of the bridge collapsing in
1769. Five people were killed. Although work was started to repair
the bridge, it was not completed until 1772. Understandably,
Edinburgh citizens were at first very reluctant to risk crossing the
new North Bridge. As work on building the New Town slowly
progressed westwards, it became more and more of an inconve-
nience for the New Town residents to access the Old Town and for
tradesmen from the Old Town to reach their wealthy customers in
their new houses. A few enterprising citizens laid planks of wood
to help them cross the muddy pools of the partially drained Nor'
Loch. However, as we saw in the case of David Hume, who lost his
footing and fell in, this could be a risky business.

There was also the problem for the builders as to what to do
with the excavated earth and stones removed to make way for the
foundations of the New Town houses. A precedent had been set
during the construction of the area around St Andrew Square. Here
the builders had simply dumped the excavated spoil at the eastern
end of the Nor' Loch. In time this was to be paved to form the

A coach of tradesmen on Geordie Boyd's Mud Brig.

present-day Waverley Bridge. It has been suggested that it was Lord Provost John Grieve who gave the green light to the builders to continue with this practice as they made their way westwards. It has been calculated that in total some 2,000,000 cartloads of spoil were dumped in the Nor' Loch to form what became known as 'The Earthen Mound'.

In 1781, George Boyd, a clothier living in Gosford's Close in the Old Town, put down planks on the Mound to make it easier for him to reach his New Town customers. For a while the Mound was nick-named 'Geordie Boyd's Mud Brig'. Here John Kay shows George Boyd as a coachman driving a team of his fellow-tradesmen from the Old Town on a coach down the 'Mud Brig' to the New Town. Provost Grieve, who had bought a new house on the corner of Hanover Street and Princes Street, added more planks to the improvised causeway. Soon a series of tracks had been laid. It has been suggested that it was Provost Grieve who was responsible for the Mound being aligned with his front door rather than with the adjacent Hanover Street.

Soon the Mound became a popular, if at times muddy, causeway. The dream of a beautiful canal separating the Old Town from the New was now lost forever. Many contemporaries were

ABOVE. A view of Hanover Street from *Modern Athens Displayed* by Thomas Shepherd, 1829. This clearly shows the Earthen Mound and some of the tracks being used. It also shows the stark contrast between the Old Town houses and those of the New Town.

OPPOSITE. James Bruce and Peter Williamson.

outraged. Henry, Lord Cockburn, a senior judge and early conservationist, wrote: 'One of the greatest mistakes committed as a matter of taste was the erection of the Earthen Mound across the beautiful valley of the loch.' There was no going back, however, and in 1834 the Mound was paved and lit.

In 1791, John Kay witnessed and recorded a remarkable confrontation between two of Edinburgh's most colourful characters. This was a fierce argument that took place outside his window between James Bruce of Kinnaird the famous explorer, and Peter Williamson, an Edinburgh shopkeeper and entrepreneur whose premises in the Luckenbooths carried a sign stating 'Peter Williamson from the other world'. So who were these men and what were they arguing about?

Kay's portrait shows Bruce and Williamson when they nearly came to blows at the site of the Mercat Cross with Williamson accusing Bruce of being an imposter. Kay may well have recorded

How dare you approach me with your travells. There is not a single word of them true
There you may be right, and altho I never dined upon the Lion oreat half a Cow and turned
the rest to grafs, yet my works have been of more use to mankind than yours
and there is more truth in one page of my Edin.r directory than in all your five
Volumes 4.o So when you talk to me dont imagine yourself at the source of the Nile.

T. Kay Del. et Sculp. Published as the Act Directs 1795

his actual exchange with Bruce. Here Williamson, on the right, is accusing Bruce of fabricating the recently published account of his expedition to Ethiopia to search for the source of the Blue Nile.

> How dare you approach me with your travels. There is not a single word of them true. There you may be right and although I never dined upon the lion or ate half a cow and turned the rest to grass yet my works have been of more use to mankind than yours and there is more truth in one page of my Edinburgh Directory than in all your five volumes quarto. So when you talk to me don't imagine yourself at the source of the Nile.

James Bruce was born in 1730 in Kinnaird House, near to Stirling. At the age of eight he was sent to London to stay with an aunt. He went to Harrow where he proved himself to be an excellent scholar. He returned to Edinburgh to study Law and entered training for the Bar, but he was not attracted to the work, much preferring a life of travel and adventure. He returned to London with a view to joining the East India Company but met Adriana Allan, fell in love and married her. He ran his father-in-law's wine business. But then tragedy struck. His expectant wife died in Paris of consumption. Bruce was distraught. He was befriended by Lord Halifax, a powerful politician who had been President of the Board of Trade. (Halifax, the capital of Nova Scotia, is named after him.) In 1763 Halifax secured him a position as Consul to the court of the Bey of Algiers. This was a very hazardous appointment as the Bey was an extremely violent and dangerous man. On his arrival, Bruce had to witness a man being strangled to death in front of him. Torture and executions occurred regularly. Bruce perhaps survived because he had a commanding physical presence. He was 6 feet 4 inches in height with a head of flaming red hair. Bruce had also gone to the trouble to learn Arabic and to dress in local costume. However, after five years Bruce had had enough.

With the permission of the British Government, Bruce managed to escape the violence of the Bey's court. He had already explored some of the ruins around Algiers and now was determined to find the source of the River Nile. He set out on his perilous adventure and 'vanished' for five years.

Bruce reached Alexandria in 1768. He was accompanied by a party of twenty porters, laden with Bruce's astronomical instruments and his Italian secretary Luigi Balugani. He reached the fabled Valley of the Kings and was the first European to enter the tomb of Ramses III. After incredible difficulties and dangers, including a shipwreck and attack by bandits, Bruce reached the court of the Ethiopian king at Gondar in 1770. Here he found even worse cruelty than he had experienced in Algiers with the mutilation of captives a regular feature of life. Ethiopia then was a country suffering from decades of bloody civil war. Bruce probably survived, because of his physical appearance; his language abilities, his skills as a self-taught doctor and the shooting power of his modern rifle. The king was clearly impressed by Bruce and appointed him as a cavalry commander and as Governor of the province of Ghish. In late 1770 he was allowed to set out on an expedition to the south of Lake Tana in search of the source of what is now known as the Blue Nile. He believed that he had indeed found the source when a marsh was pointed out to him by a local guide. (In fact Bruce had missed the real source close by at Lake Tana.)

Bruce left Gondar in December 1771. On his way back to Cairo he became the first European to discover the confluence of the Blue Nile with the White Nile. His journey through the desert was a terrible ordeal. Some of his party including Balugani had died in Ethiopia; others now perished from heat exhaustion and thirst. Bruce somehow survived and arrived in Cairo in January 1773 and sailed for France which he reached in March. He was well-received by Louis XVI. He then travelled to Italy seeking a long-lost girlfriend only to find that she had married during his long absence. He at last got back to Britain in 1774 and had an audience with George III. His account though was dismissed by most as a fantasy adventure. Many, including Dr Samuel Johnson, refused to believe his description of his travels, the cruelty of the court and the lives of the people.

He returned to Kinnaird, married and had a family but he did not publish an account of his adventures, *Travels to Discover the Source of the Nile, In the Years 1768, 1769, 1770, 1771, 1772 and 1773*, until after the death of his wife in 1790. The work comprised five large volumes which, as well as Bruce's extraordinary adventures, also included an account of the history of Ethiopia. In addition there was a further volume published which was filled with maps and pictures of birds, plants and animals drawn during the expedition. Most still refused to believe him. Bruce was a disappointed and embittered man. He remarked to his daughter:

> The world is strangely mistaken in my character, by supposing that I would condescend to write a romance for its amusement. I shall not live to witness it but you probably will see the truth of all I have written and decisively confirmed.

However, Bruce was right. Future expeditions were to confirm much of what Bruce had described in his books. In addition, he had returned with a collection of manuscripts, artefacts and his own drawings. These created a great interest both in Ancient Egypt, the sources of the River Nile and the ancient kingdom of Gondar, now Ethiopia.

Bruce entertained on a lavish scale at Kinnaird House. He often dressed in Ethiopian robes. These were to prove his downfall. At the end of a large supper party held in 1794, Bruce had escorted one group of his guests to their carriage. He started up the stairs to escort another when his foot caught in his robe and he fell striking his head. He never regained consciousness and died the next day.

Amongst the doubters was Peter Williamson, whose own remarkable story almost defies belief. Peter Williamson was born in Aberdeenshire about 1735. He was staying with an aunt in Aberdeen when he was kidnapped at the harbour and along with a group of other unfortunate children, he was shipped across to America to be sold as a slave. He was only eight years old. Their boat was wrecked off the coast of Delaware but Williamson survived. He was lucky in that he was bought by a Mr Wilson, another Scot who had himself been kidnapped when a boy in Perth. Williamson worked hard for his master and in return was well-treated and educated. Mr Wilson died leaving Williamson £120 (equivalent to about £16,000 today). With this money Williamson was able to marry and to purchase land in Pennsylvania. He was not to enjoy his happiness for long. In 1753 he was seized by a raiding party of Cherokee native Americans. His house and crops were destroyed and his animals killed. Williamson witnessed the massacre and scalping of several other settler families as the raiding party returned to their village. Williamson was very badly treated but managed to escape in 1754. He was chased for several days but was able to out-run his pursuers.

After a series of hair-raising adventures, he made his way back to Pennsylvania. Williamson enlisted in the volunteer army that was being raised to fight the invading French and their native American allies but was captured in a skirmish. He was released in 1756 and eventually made his way back to England. He was destitute when he arrived in Plymouth. Williamson was able to beg his way to York. There he published an account of his adventures. This made him enough money to travel north to Aberdeen as he was convinced that the Council there had connived at the kidnapping of children. Needless to say, Aberdeen Council were not best pleased. Williamson was arrested and convicted of libelling the Council. The offending pages were torn from copies of his book and burned at the Mercat Cross by the public hangman. Williamson was forced out of Aberdeen. Others though confirmed his claims of abduction and took up Williamson's case. Williamson appealed his sentence and the verdict was overturned; he was eventually awarded £200 damages and costs against Aberdeen Council.

Williamson now moved to Edinburgh where he reprinted his book which exposed the scandal of the kidnapping of children in several Scottish towns to be sold as slaves across the Atlantic. Williamson married again and opened Peter's Tavern and one of Edinburgh's first Coffee Houses in Parliament Close just across from Kay's workshop. He also opened a shop in the Luckenbooths where he produced Edinburgh's first Street Directory in 1775. This was sold for 1/- (5p). Amongst the entries for June 1775 to June 1776 we have mention of Deacon William Brodie living in Brodie's Close. The volume for June 1786 to June 1788 includes: 'John Kay, Engraver near the Cross' (the site of the old Mercat Cross). He also published a weekly paper, *The Scots Spy or Critical Observer*. In 1779 Williamson started Edinburgh's first 'Penny Post'. He employed four men to do the deliveries who were paid 4/6d (22.5p) a week. Letters were to be left at collection points located around the burgh with several deliveries being promised daily. By now he was something of a celebrity, and known as 'Indian Peter'. On occasions he would dress up in a Cherokee costume and delighted children by doing a

Mr Peter Williamson *in the Dress of a* Delaware Indian, *with his* Tomohawk, Scalping knife, &c.

war dance with native American war cries. He died in 1799 and is buried in Edinburgh's Calton Burial Ground. We do not know whether Bruce and Williamson ever spoke to each other again after their argument in 1791.

Did John Kay ever cause such offence with his portraits as to get himself into trouble? We are told that Kay was once assaulted in the street by an individual who disliked his portrait. On another occasion he was taken to Court by two Edinburgh citizens angered that Kay had drawn a bet that the two had made. This was a wager made between Hamilton Bell, an Edinburgh lawyer and Edward Innes, a baker and confectioner. Like many of his fellow Edinburgh lawyers, Bell conducted much of his business in a tavern. He would arrange to meet his clients in Fortune's Tavern in the Old Stamp Office Close just down the High Street from the home of John Kay. Bell was also a member of the Cape Club which met in Fortune's and thus would have known Deacon Brodie, who was also a member of the Club. Bell was a tall, well-built man who was proud of his physical strength. Over drinks one evening he bet his friend Innes to a walking race from Edinburgh to Musselburgh and back – a distance of some 12 miles (17 km). To prove his strength, Bell would carry a boy upon his back. The pair agreed to set off just after dawn to avoid the ridicule of any onlookers. Each had a companion to carry bottles to quench their thirst. We do not know whether they were filled with water or something stronger.

In the illustration on page 138 Kay has drawn Bell striding out with young Charles Osman, a vintner's boy, on his back. (Osman was to become the first proprietor of the Waterloo Hotel which stood at the approach to Waterloo Place.) He is accompanied by Mr John Rae, a dentist. They are passing two fishwives on their way from Fisherrow, a little fishing village on the outskirts of Musselburgh, to Edinburgh with their creels of freshly caught fish on their backs. In a separate image (page 139) Kay shows a clearly flagging Innes accompanied by his friend Mr James Cooper, a jeweller.

Kay's portraits of the race caused much amusement. However, while Innes and Cooper were prepared to laugh it off, Bell and Rae

OPPOSITE. A contemporary print of Peter Williamson or 'Indian Peter'.

ABOVE. Mr Hamilton Bell carrying Charles Osman on his back accompanied by Mr John Rae.

OPPOSITE TOP. Mr Innes accompanied by Mr Rae.

OPPOSITE BOTTOM. John Kay pleading his case before Sheriff Pringle. He has deliberately made Hamilton Bell and John Rae look ridiculous.

decided to sue Kay for defamation. The case was heard by Sheriff John Pringle. Kay defended himself and was quickly able to establish that the men had indeed made a bet and that he was only recording an event that had actually happened. The case against Kay was thrown out. Kay got his revenge by drawing the scene. Here he stands in front of Sheriff Pringle while Bell and Rae, drawn in very unflattering poses, are depicted with looks of outrage on their faces. Kay meantime is the picture of composure and self-restraint.

J. Kay fecit 1792

1792   Examination.

CHAPTER 12

Portraits of some Visitors
to Edinburgh

John Kay drew portraits of a considerable number of visitors to Edinburgh. This could well have been a commercial decision as, without illustrated newspapers, Kay must have believed there would be sufficient interest in buying a print of a celebrity by way of a souvenir. It is apparent from Kay's surviving portraits that there must have been a steady stream of individuals who were either exceptionally tall like the three Irish giants shown opposite, or exceptionally small. These people earned a living by exhibiting themselves to the paying public. Here Kay shows three visiting Irishmen on display with several local characters, including the engraver Andrew Bell, beside them.

Another character who visited Edinburgh to attract customers was Dr James Graham, the creator of London's celebrated 'Temple of Health and Hymen'. Dr Graham was in fact a native of Edinburgh having been born in the Cowgate in 1745. Having completed his medical studies at the university, Dr Graham practised in England. After some years, however, he went to the American colonies where he built up a reputation as a hard-working and caring doctor.

On the outbreak of the American War of Independence, Graham returned to his native Edinburgh. It was around this time that he realised the opportunities that existed in the field of sexual advice for gentlemen. We must appreciate that there was a profound ignorance amongst the adult population concerning physical relationships between the sexes. Dr Graham set out to remedy this.

The Three Irish Giants.

He moved to London and there opened his 'Temple of Venus and Hymen' in the Pall Mall. This was a lavishly decorated and scented hall where for the price of 3/- (15p) gentlemen could attend lectures by Dr Graham. These lectures were for 'preventing barrenness, and propagating a much more strong, beautiful, active, healthy, wise, and virtuous race of human beings . . .' Dr Graham certainly went in for some fairly sensational advertising:

> If there be one human being, rich or poor, male, female, or of the doubtful gender [this would appear to be a remarkable acknowledgement of the existence of lesbian, gay and transgender individuals in society?], in or near this great

Dr Graham and a lady crossing the North Bridge. Several of Kay's portraits
are set here on the bridge usually with an obvious wind blowing.

metropolis of the world, who has not had the good fortune
and happiness of hearing the celebrated lecture, and of
seeing the grand celestial state bed, the magnificent electrical
apparatus, and the supremely afterwards brilliant and
unique decorations of this magical edifice, of this enchanting
Elysian palace! – where wit and mirth, love and beauty – all
that can delight the soul, and all that can ravish the senses –
will hold their court, this, and every evening this week, in
chaste and joyous assemblage! Let them now come forth, or
for ever [sic] afterwards let them blame themselves, and
bewail their irremediable misfortune.

Dr Graham lecturing to a packed audience in Edinburgh.

Those who ventured to enter the Temple were greeted by a column on which stood a very scantily clad young woman posing as Venus. This was in fact Amy Lyon who later changed her name to Emma Hart. She became the mistress of Sir William Hamilton, marrying him in London in 1791 when she was twenty-six and he was sixty. The couple moved to Naples where in 1793, Emma met Admiral Nelson. The pair became lovers, and in 1801 Emma gave birth to their daughter, Horatia. Emma died in poverty in France in 1815.

For an additional charge, customers could climb into the bed where they received an electric shock supposedly to improve their sexual performance. Naturally this attracted the disapproval of the

NINTY FOUR YEARS HAVE I
SOJOURNED UPON THIS EARTH
ENDEAVOURING TO DO GOOD

authorities and in 1783, Dr Graham returned to his native Edinburgh. Here he advertised his notorious course of lectures. Dr Graham was arrested and imprisoned in the Tolbooth. He was fined £20 and ordered to be detained until the fine was paid. He was soon released, however, and with so many Edinburgh gentlemen eager to hear Dr Graham, his fine was quickly paid. Dr Graham gave several lectures but it seems that later in 1783, he had something of a breakdown. He was declared insane in 1788 and died in 1794. He too is buried in Greyfriars Kirkyard.

In 1790 the Methodist preacher John Wesley visited Edinburgh for the last time. He had made several visits to Scotland where he preached in the open air. Unlike his experience of preaching in England, however, he seems to have had little success in converting the Calvinist Scots. He recorded his frustration thus: 'O! What a difference between the living stones and the dead, unfeeling multitudes of Scotland.'

John Kay drew the 84-year-old (not 94 as stated in the portrait) Dr Wesley walking down the High Street from the Castlehill where he had preached his last outdoor sermon. He is supported on his right by Dr James Hamilton, born in Dunbar, who had served as a surgeon in the Royal Navy before converting to Methodism and a fellow-Methodist preacher the Reverend Joseph Cole.

One of the most colourful characters to visit Edinburgh drawn by John Kay was the Italian balloonist Vincenzo Lunardi. He arrived in Edinburgh in 1785 and on 5 October of that year made a balloon ascent from the grounds of Heriot's Hospital. A crowd of 80,000 gathered to witness the event. At noon a flag was raised from Edinburgh Castle and a gun was fired at the scene. The balloon was inflated and at 2.45pm rose into the air. The wind took Lunardi out over the Firth of Forth and past the island of Inchkeith. From there he was carried over North Berwick and then across the Forth to land in a field near Ceres. The local minister, the Reverend Arnot, had to rescue him from a crowd of terrified farm workers who were preparing to kill him with their scythes thinking that he was a devil. He was feted with a dinner in Cupar and next day awarded with an

OPPOSITE. John Wesley supported by two friends.

ABOVE. Vincenzo Lunardi's first Edinburgh flight.

honorary membership of the Royal & Ancient Golf Club in St Andrews. A contemporary account described the flight:

> The beauty and grandeur of the spectacle could only be exceeded by the cool, intrepid manner in which the adventurer conducted himself; and indeed he seemed infinitely more at ease than the greater part of his spectators.

However, this was not the first balloon flight in Scotland, nor indeed in the United Kingdom. On 27 August 1784, James Tytler, an eccentric Edinburgh author, made a short flight of a few hundred feet in a fire balloon launched in the present-day Queen's Park. Other attempts failed. His flight beat Lunardi's first flight in London by a month.

La. RAN. Eternal providence ! What is thy name ?
My name is NORVAL : and my name he bears.
DOUGLAS
J.Kayfect. 1784

Mrs Siddons playing the character of Lady Randolph in Hume's tragedy *Douglas*.

Tytler was chronically in debt. He had edited the second and third editions of *The Encyclopaedia Britannica* after working as a minister, a doctor and a ship's surgeon. His radical political views got him into trouble with the authorities and he eventually fled to the United States of America where he died in 1804.

Lunardi meantime made four other flights in Scotland including another in Edinburgh. He was very full of himself and boasted of his reputation with the young ladies of Edinburgh. He once toasted himself as: 'Lunardi, whom the ladies love'. The Lunardi Bonnet became fashionable and is mentioned by Burns in his poem 'Tae a Louse'. Lunardi died in Italy in 1809.

Edinburgh's Theatre Royal opened in Shakespeare Square at the east end of Princes Street in 1769. Many well-known actors performed here, including Mrs Sarah Siddons, John Kemble and Edmund Kean. In the portrait above Kay has drawn Mrs Siddons in the role of Lady Randolph in Hume's tragedy *Douglas*. Clearly Edinburgh

Sir Walter Scott.

theatre-goers were hard to please. Mrs Siddons' first appearance on stage was met by silence from the Edinburgh audience which seriously disturbed the famous actress. She threw everything she had into her next scene to more silence and then a voice called out 'That's no' bad', which provoked a storm of laughter and thunderous applause. For her next appearance there were 2,557 applications for 630 places and troops were required to quell the crush to get tickets. She was paid the staggering sum of £200 (equivalent to about £21,000 today) per night.

While we are indebted to John Kay for the many portraits that he drew and engraved, there are some striking omissions from his published work. For example, there is no Professor Adam Ferguson, no Provost William Creech, no James Boswell, no Robert Adam, and only a small cameo of Walter Scott drawn alongside a group of fellow lawyers.

Other notable absentees include the artists Sir Henry Raeburn and Alexander Nasmyth. And there is no Robert Burns. Perhaps their plates were lost or destroyed; perhaps, for whatever reason, Kay elected not to draw them. It is unlikely that we shall ever know the reasons for their absence. Certainly in the case of Robert Burns it is not unreasonable to surmise that there would have been a ready market to obtain a print of the celebrity poet.

Burns first started writing serious poetry, mostly in Scots, in 1785. To this year belong such gems as 'Holy Willie's Prayer', 'The Cotter's Saturday Night' and 'The Address to a Mouse'. Poverty, however, was never far away from Burns. In 1786 he had been on the point of emigrating to Jamaica when he was persuaded by his friends to have some of his poems published. The success of the *Kilmarnock Edition* of his poems persuaded him to visit Edinburgh, where another edition of his poems was printed. Burns left for the capital on a borrowed pony and arrived in Edinburgh on 28

OPPOSITE. Miss Margaret Burns.

THE *British Antiquarian*

November 1786. He took up residence in the lodgings of his Ayrshire friend John Richmond in Baxter's Close in the Lawnmarket.

Burns swept Edinburgh off its feet and even the doors of titled families were open in welcome to the 'Ploughman Poet' as he was styled. Here is how his arrival struck one contemporary, Mrs Alison Cockburn. She wrote to a friend:

> The whole town is at present agog with the ploughman poet, who receives adulation with native dignity . . . He has seen Duchess Gordon and all the gay world.

However, while we do not have a Kay portrait of Robert Burns, John Kay certainly drew two visitors to Edinburgh who were well known to Burns.

Miss Margaret Burns was a noted beauty who was born in Durham in 1769. In 1789 she moved to Edinburgh and took up residence in Rose Street in the New Town. As chance would have it, she was a near-neighbour of William Creech, the famous publisher and future Lord Provost. Creech had a reputation for being something of a prude. So he was not impressed by the arrival of his attractive young neighbour.

Miss Burns immediately attracted attention by parading along Princes Street dressed in the height of fashion, which at that time meant a very low neckline. Miss Burns was also in the habit of entertaining her boyfriends in her house, much to the annoyance of Creech. He actually had Miss Burns brought before the Burgh Court demanding that she be banished from the city. Creech himself presided over the case and had her sentenced to six months in gaol and to be banished thereafter from Edinburgh. However, Miss Burns was not going to give up without a fight. She had plenty of admirers, including Robert Burns. In her defence he wrote:

> Cease ye prudes, your envious railing.
> Lovely Burns has charms – confess;
> True it is she had one failing –
> Had a woman ever less?

OPPOSITE. Francis Grose.

The case was thrown out on appeal and Creech was widely ridiculed. Adverts appeared in newspapers announcing his engagement to Miss Burns. However, she decided that Edinburgh was too narrow-minded for a woman of her spirit. She moved to nearby Lasswade but sadly died there of consumption in 1792, aged only twenty-three.

Francis Grose, 'The British Antiquarian', was born in 1731. After a brief military career followed by spells in the militia where he got heavily into debt, Grose decided to further his interest in the past. He toured England and Wales noting down and sketching historical old buildings and ruins. Between 1772 and 1776, he published the four volumes of his *Antiquities of England*.

Grose then turned his attention to Scotland. He made his first visit in 1788 and returned the following year and spent several months in Edinburgh. Grose was indeed very overweight as he is shown by Kay (page 150) but he laughed it off. While in Edinburgh, Grose met again with Robert Burns, whom he had first met in Dumfriesshire. The two became very good friends – and drinking companions – with Burns giving Grose much useful advice about the antiquities of Ayrshire for the planned book on Scotland. Grose was extremely grateful and promised to dedicate the book to Robert Burns if he would write a short piece about his native Ayrshire. Both men kept their side of the bargain. In his dedication to *The Antiquities of Scotland* published posthumously in 1797, Grose recorded his gratitude to Burns:

> To my ingenious friend Mr. Robert Burns, I have been very much obligated: he not only was at the pains of making out what was most worthy of note in Ayrshire, the county honoured by his birth, but he also wrote, expressly for this work, the pretty tale annexed to Alloway Church.

'The pretty tale' referred to by Grose was of course *Tam o' Shanter*. Grose left for a tour of Ireland but died there in 1791 aged sixty.

CHAPTER 13

'Such are our Manners in Scotland'

In 1773 the famous Edinburgh poet Robert Fergusson published 'Auld Reekie', a colourful description of his home town. This poem, and others penned by Fergusson, confirm the impression that, while Edinburgh might be enjoying an international reputation for its intellectual genius, there was quite another life being enjoyed by many of the citizens once the day's work was done.

> Now night that's cunzied chief for fun,   [considered]
> Is with her usual rites begun . . .
> Some to porter, some to punch,
> Retire; while noisy ten-hours' drum
> Gars a' the trades gang danderin' hame.   [strolling]
> Now many a club, jocose and free,   [friendly]
> Gi'e a' to merriment and glee;
> Wi' sang and glass they fley the power   [drive off]
> O' care that wad harass the hour.
>
> (Robert Fergusson, 'Auld Reekie')

There would appear to have been quite a few clubs 'jocose and free' to be found in the Old Town. Robert Chambers in his *Traditions of Edinburgh* lists several of them, including the Pious Club – the club's name alluded to the members meeting in a pie-house; the Spendthrift Club – the club's name alluded to the members not being allowed to spend more than 4½d (2p) on entertainment each night; the Boar Club – the Club's members were 'wild, fashionable young

Retaliation; or the Cudgeller Caught

An assault in an Edinburgh street, drawn by John Kay.

men' who grunted like pigs; the Sweating Club – after a heavy
night's drinking, the club members would roam the streets looking
for unfortunate victims to chase and to assault; the Facer Club – a
member who could not finish his drink had to throw it in his face;
the Horn Order – a fashionable drinking club where men and
women would meet in disguise; and the notorious Hell-Fire Club

– 'A terrible and infamous association of wild young men'.

John Kay perhaps might have been a member of the Crochallan Fencibles, a club which met in Dawney Douglas's tavern down Anchor Close, just next to Kay's home on the High Street. The club was named after a Gaelic song *Cro Chalien* ('Colin's Cattle') regularly sung by the landlord. Notable members of this club included the printer William Smellie whose workshop was slightly further down Anchor Close. Smellie introduced Robert Burns to the club. Burns described Smellie sitting drinking in the tavern exchanging banter with his companions:

> Yet though his caustic wit was biting, rude
> His heart was warm, benevolent and good.

Just further down the High Street, in the Old Stamp Office Close, was another club, the Cape Club. The club was originally founded in the 1700s but not formally constituted until 1764. Its insignia were a cape, or crown, worn by the Sovereign of the Cape, and two maces in the form of huge steel pokers. When a new Knight of the Cape was inaugurated he was led forward by his sponsors, and kneeling before the Sovereign, had to grasp the poker and take an oath of fidelity, while all Knights stood with Pokers raised to acknowledge acceptance:

> I devoutly swear by this light, to be a true and faithful knight,
> with all my might, both day and night, so help me Poker!

Among the more famous members of the original Cape Club was Deacon William Brodie, a leading Edinburgh citizen who in 1788 was to be arrested, tried and sentenced to death for attempting to rob the Excise Office in Chessel's Court in the Canongate.

It is certainly true that Brodie did lead something of a double life – the upright and respectable citizen by day and the villain by night. However, contemporary descriptions of the social life in Edinburgh at that time would suggest that there were many more of Brodie's fellow-citizens whose behavior involved a fair degree of double-standards and hypocrisy. Brodie's misfortune was to be tempted into robbery to fund his extravagances.

We have already encountered the Edinburgh lawyer Hugo Arnot

in Chapter 8 despairing of what he saw as a dramatic decline in standards of behaviour in Edinburgh between 1763 and 1783. Clearly fear of the disapproval of the Church of Scotland had waned. While there was still an expectation that people would attend at least one of the Sunday services, the conduct of many of them suggests that they succumbed to the temptations that surrounded them. Heavy drinking was a long-standing problem in Edinburgh. An English visitor to the burgh writing in 1578 commented that: 'the excess of drinking was then far greater among the Scots that the English'. Heavy drinking was still very much a part of life in 18th-century Edinburgh.

James Boswell, the biographer of Dr Samuel Johnson, kept a secret journal in which he recorded what he had been doing each day. His journal along with his other private papers was only discovered in Malahide Castle north of Dublin in the 1920s. His journal has subsequently been published in several volumes by Yale University. Some of the entries make shocking reading. The supposedly God-fearing Boswell is revealed as a hard-drinking womaniser who fathered at least two illegitimate children and suffered from chronic venereal disease. Here is part of the entry for Saturday 30 July 1774:

> My head was inflamed and confused considerably. However I went to the Parliament House a little after nine. I found the Solicitor-General [Henry Dundas, the future Viscount Melville], who had been with us last night and drank heartily standing in the Outer Hall looking very ill . . . In some countries being seen in such a state would be thought shocking. Such are our manners in Scotland that it is nothing at all.

Hugo Arnot, describing the behaviour of young men at Edinburgh's Dancing Assembly in 1783, commented that:

> Dress particularly by the men, is much neglected; and many of them reel from the tavern, flustered with wine, to an assembly of as elegant and beautiful women as any in Europe.

On 28 August 1776, Boswell recorded that:

The Hon. Henry Erskine [the defence advocate for William Brodie] and I drove out to Dreghorn, where we had a party at bowls . . . I drank too much. We had whist after dinner. When I returned to town I was a good deal intoxicated, ranged the streets and having met with a comely, fresh-looking girl, madly ventured to be with her on the north brae of the Castle Hill. I told my dear wife immediately.

Poor Mrs Boswell had to endure many such confessions from her feckless husband.

Hugo Arnot meantime was dismayed at the sudden rise in the number of prostitutes plying their trade on the streets of Edinburgh.

In 1763 there were about six or seven brothels or houses of bad fame in Edinburgh and very few only of the lowest and most ignorant order of females skulked about at night. A person might have walked from the Castle Hill to the Abbey [Holyrood] without being accosted by a single prostitute.

In 1783 the number of brothels are increased to some hundreds and the women of the town are more than is equal in proportion. Every quarter of the city and suburbs is infested with multitudes of females abandoned to vice and many of them before passion could mislead or reason teach them right from wrong. Some mothers live by the prostitution of their daughters. Gentlemen's and citizen's daughters are upon the town, who by their dress and bold deportment, in the face of the day, seem to tell us that the term WH – – E ceases to be a reproach.

For visitors to Edinburgh, *The Directory of Ladies of Pleasure in Edinburgh* (1775), allegedly compiled by James Tytler, describes the charms of sixty-six such ladies. Here is a typical entry:

Miss Peggy Bruce at Miss Walker's

This lady is about twenty years of age, rather short, fair hair and complexion, good teeth, fine eyes and skin and very

good natured. She is a most devout worshipper at the Shrine
of Venus and let her lover be ever so vigorous she will not
be a motion behind hand in performing the amorous fate.
Take her all together, she is not a bad pennyworth for any
gentleman.

It is reckoned that there were over two hundred brothels in the
town. There was also trouble on the streets as those brave enough
to venture out after dark were liable to be assaulted by young men
out looking for trouble.

This day the magistrates fined a number of young men for
rioting on the streets of this metropolis on the evening of
Sunday past.

(*Edinburgh Evening Courant,* 10 January 1788)

That same day Thomas Elliot and James Alexander were
whipped through the city in pursuance of a sentence of the
magistrates having been convicted of wantonly knocking
down people on the streets. Notwithstanding the late
examples that have been made of people guilty of such
nefarious practices for which great praise is certainly due to
our Magistrates, we are sorry to observe the little impression
this degree of punishment has made upon the wretched
banditti, who infest our streets; as no longer ago that last
Saturday evening an industrious tradesman, returning from
his lawful employment, was knocked down, beat, bruised,
and otherwise maltreated about the head of Forrester's
Wynd, for which no reason can be given but the wanton
wickedness of the perpetrators.

(*Edinburgh Evening Courant,* 13 March 1788)

Gambling was another problem. There were regular gatherings of
men to play at cards and dice. The most notorious gambling den
was to be found at James Clark's Tavern in Fleshmarket Close, just
a few metres down from John Kay's High Street home. Deacon
Brodie was a regular visitor. Others bet large sums on cock-fighting.
   Kay drew a famous cock-fight that took place in 1785 in the
partially completed kitchen of the new Assembly Rooms, then

Thus we poor Cooks, exert our Skill & Brav'ry
For idle Gulls, and Kites, that trade in Knav'ry

The cock-fight held in the partially built Assembly Rooms, George Street, in 1785.

under construction in the New Town's George Street. He included several recognisable characters among the spectators, including Deacon William Brodie.

Edinburgh was about to experience a spate of housebreakings and robberies that were to baffle the authorities. Did any of those gathered for that cock-fight ever suspect that their fellow-gambler, William Brodie, was leading a double-life?

CHAPTER 14

The Story of
Deacon Brodie

On 14 January 1788, an unusual advertisement was placed in the *Edinburgh Evening Courant*:

> The frequency of housebreaking of late in this place should make people carefully to examine their doors and windows which in general are very carelessly and insufficiently secured. Shops, in particular, which contain articles of value, should have something more than a single lock which is easily picked, to secure them.

For months Edinburgh had suffered a series of baffling burglaries. There rarely was any sign of a forced entrance; the robberies usually took place when the premises were empty and the robbers seemed to know exactly where to look for any valuables. Only once was one of the robbers spotted when an elderly lady, confined to bed through illness, was startled to see a man dressed in black entering her room. The man, seeing the lady, bowed his head and left. The lady thought that it looked like her neighbour Deacon Brodie but she dismissed this as a ridiculous idea. Despite the warnings, the robberies continued unchecked. Readers of the *Edinburgh Evening Courant* were treated to a steady stream of reports of yet more break-ins.

A robbery at the Gingerbread Baker in Exchequer Row. Everything was carried off.

The Entrance to Brodie's Close, Lawnmarket.

Last night the shop of Thomas Allan & Co, Grocers on the shore of Leith was broken in . . . A reward of twenty guineas is offered . . .

The most spectacular robbery occurred in January 1788 when a leading shop was broken into:

That this last night the shop of Messrs Inglis, Horner and Co, Silk Merchants, was broken into . . . the value of the goods stolen is equal to £400–£500. A reward of £100 is offered.

A large advertisement was placed in the *Courant* offering a substantial reward for information leading to the arrest and conviction of the thieves. It also promised a pardon to anyone willing to turn King's Evidence against their fellow criminals. It was this advertisement that was to bring Deacon Brodie to the scaffold.

Deacon William Brodie had been born in 1741 in the family home in Brodie's Close on the south side of the Lawnmarket. He was the eldest of eleven children. His father, Francis Brodie, had run a successful business as a builder and carpenter. He had been appointed as the Deacon of Edinburgh's Incorporation of Wrights and Masons and sat as a Deacon Councillor on the Town Council. On his death, William inherited his father's property, his successful business and, it was claimed at his trial, the considerable sum of £10,000 (equivalent to more than £1,300,000 today). In time he too became the Deacon of the Wrights and Masons and as such a member of the Town Council.

To most of his fellow-citizens he must have appeared as a wealthy, successful businessman. He was married with three children and was considered to be one of the most fashionably dressed men in the burgh. There were, however, a few who knew that Brodie was leading a double life. He was a serial gambler with two mistresses, Jean Watt in nearby Libberton's Wynd and Ann Grant who lived near to John Kay's house in Cant's Close. By these women, Brodie had fathered a further five children. Furthermore he had gambled away his fortune, and by 1786, he faced the threat of his debtors insisting on payment. The fear for Brodie was that as well as the shame of public exposure, there was the real prospect of he and his family being locked up in the debtors' prison.

It would appear that Brodie turned to crime sometime in 1786 when he met George Smith, a convicted housebreaker from London, who was on the run from a sentence of transportation. (However, there are claims that Brodie had been housebreaking for several years before this.) They shared an interest in gambling and it could well have been in Clark's Tavern that the two first met. For the next eighteen months Edinburgh experienced that wave of house and shop-breaking that so baffled the authorities. It was only during the subsequent trial of Brodie and Smith that their methods were revealed. As the employer of several tradesmen, Brodie could quite

SHOP-BREAKING AND THEFT.

SHERIFF-CLERK'S OFFICE, EDINBURGH, JAN. 9. 1788.

THAT this laſt night the ſhop of Meſſ. INGLIS, HORNER, and Co. Silk Mercers at the Croſs of Edinburgh, was broke into, and the following articles ſtolen and carried off therefrom, viz.

A conſiderable quantity of black luteſtrings, black armozeens, black florentines, and raſdimore ſilks, ſome of them whole, others cut pieces. Moſt of the armozeens and luteſtrings have yellow liſts or ſelveges, with ſome red threads on the outer edge ; others of the luteſtrings, and all the florentines, have white ſelveges. All of the ſilks were rol'ed on pins or blocks, upon the end of moſt of which is the following mark, I. I . S. with the number of the piece, and quantity of the yards, in figures—Several pieces of cambric, ſome whole, ſome cut— Alſo a piece of plain white ſattin. It is more than probable that the ſaid goods may be cut in ſuch a manner as to cauſe them, when expoſed to ſale, to have the appearance of remnants.

The value of the above goods is equal to from 400l. to 500l. Sterling. ſo far as yet diſcovered.

Whoever will give to William Scott, procurator-fiſcal of this county, within three months from this date, ſuch information as ſhall be the means of leading to a diſcovery of the perſon or perſons who committed the aforeſaid ſhop-breaking and theft, or will cauſe apprehend and impriſon the ſaid perſon or perſons, ſhall, upon conviction of the offender or offenders, receive a Reward of ONE HUNDRED POUNDS Sterling, and the informer's name, if required, concealed.

N. B. If articles, ſimilar to thoſe above deſcribed, are offered to ſale or diſcovered in the cuſtody of any perſon of a ſuſpicious appearance, it is intreated that the goods may be ſtopped, and the perſon or perſons in whoſe cuſtody they are found ſecured, till notice is ſent as above ; for which a handſome reward will be given, beſides all charges paid.

The January 1788 *Edinburgh Evening Courant* advertisement.

legitimately visit them at their work. The Edinburgh practice then was to hang your keys on a peg by your front door. All Brodie had to do was to carry a lump of putty or wax in his pocket to take an impression of the keys and to have duplicate keys made. Indeed a quantity of such keys was presented as evidence at the trial.

Kay's portrait shows the two men in discussion. Brodie is very fashionably dressed with his tricorn (or cocked) hat, fob chain and

The First Interview in 1786

Duplicate keys and a lantern owned by Deacon Brodie.

silver-buckled shoes. Kay often included something topical or humorous in his portraits so here he has shown a spurred fighting cock between the two men.

In February 1788, Brodie learnt that some £600 (equivalent to about £70,000 today) was to be lodged in the Excise Office in Chessel's Court in the Canongate. He and Smith managed to get an impression of the outer office door key but not the inner. The door would have to be broken down. This was going to be a big job so Brodie and Smith recruited Andrew Ainslie, an Edinburgh thief and John Brown, alias Humphrey Moore, another English thief on the run from justice. On the night of 5 March 1788, the four men met in Brodie's workshop in Brodie's Close and put on dark clothing. Brodie reputedly was in fine spirits and sang the Highwaymen's Song from the popular musical *The Beggar's Opera* by John Gay. (By a coincidence the opera was to be performed in Edinburgh that May.)

> Let us take the road.
> Hark! I hear the sound of coaches!
> The hour of attack approaches,
> To your arms, brave boys, and load.
> See the ball I hold!

OPPOSITE. George Smith and Deacon Brodie.

The robbery was a disaster. With Ainslie watching the entrance from the Canongate and Brodie watching the outer door, Brown and Smith broke their way into the inner office.

They were surprised by the return of Mr James Bonnar, the Deputy-Solicitor who had left some papers in the outer office. Bonnar lived just across the courtyard of Chessel's Court so had not been noticed by Ainslie watching at the street entrance. Ainslie and Brodie fled leaving Brown and Smith waiting anxiously with their pistols cocked. When Bonnar left, they too fled the scene taking only some £16 in notes and coins. The robbers met up in Brodie's workshop and then parted to get alibis for themselves. Brodie went to the home of Jean Watt, one of his mistresses. The robbery was not discovered until the next morning. Brown, taking advantage of the amnesty offered for the earlier robbery handed himself into the authorities. At first he only named Ainslie and Smith who were quickly arrested. Brodie visited them in the Tolbooth to see whether they would inform on him. Brown then made a second statement, this time naming Brodie as the leader of the gang. Brodie fled. You can imagine the shock when this advertisement appeared in the *Courant*.

12 March 1788 Sheriff Clerk's Office – £200 Reward

Whereas William Brodie, a considerable House Carpenter and Burgess of the City of Edinburgh has been charged with being concerned in the breaking into the General Excise Office for Scotland and stealing from the Cashier's Office a sum of money – and as the said William Brodie has either made his escape from Edinburgh or is still concealed about that place – a Reward of £150 is offered for his capture alone and a further £50 for his conviction.

There then followed an interesting description of the fugitive:

William Brodie is about five feet four inches. He is about forty-eight years of age but looks rather younger than he is. Broad of the shoulders and very small over the loins – has dark brown full eyes with large black eyebrows – under the right eye is the scar of a cut – a sallow complexion –

black hair, twisted, tied up behind, coming far down on each cheek, and the whiskers very sandy at the end: high topped at the front and frizzed at the side – high, smooth forehead – has a particular air in his walk, takes long steps, strikes the ground – usually wears a stick underhand and moves in a proud, swaggering sort of stile [sic] – his legs small above the ancle [sic], large ancle [sic] bones and a large foot, small at the knee which bend when he walks as if through weakness. Was dressed in a black coat, vest, breeches and stockings, a striped duffle great coat and silver shoe buckle.

(*Edinburgh Evening Courant*, 12 March 1788)

The paper was not slow to comment on the significance of the arrest of Ainslie and Smith and the flight of Brodie.

The depredations that have been committed by house-breakers in and about this city for this sometime past have been no less alarming, than the art by which they are executed, and the concealment that has attended them, have been surprising . . . From a discovery however just made, there is reason to hope that a stop will soon be put to such acts of atrocious villainy. With what amazement must it strike every friend of virtue and honesty to find that a person is charged with a crime of the above nature who very lately held a distinguished rank among his fellow citizens . . .? For what other than avarice can we impute the late robbery committed upon the Excise Office when the situation of the supposed perpetrator is considered? No excuse from necessity can be pled for a man [Brodie] in the enjoyment of thousands, who will run the risk of life, honour and reputation in order to attain the unlawful possession of what could in a trifling degree add to his supposed happiness.

(*Edinburgh Evening Courant*, 13 March 1788)

Brodie had disappeared. George Williamson, the King's Messenger for Scotland, set off on his trail but lost Brodie in London. Meantime, back in Edinburgh, John Brown was assisting the authorities. The *Courant* for 17 March 1788 reported that:

Yesterday upon information of one of the parties concerned in the late shop-breakings [John Brown] a number of keys and other implements were found concealed in different places around the city.

Brodie's premises and house were searched and a number of incriminating items were found including loaded pistols, false keys and burglary tools. In May, Ainslie and Smith made a desperate attempt to escape from the Tolbooth:

Last night or early this morning an attempt was made to break the prison of this city. Smith and Ainslie who stand charged with several shop-breakings, having taken the iron hoops of two buckets which stood in the room and formed them into saws, with these and the handles of the buckets, they made shift to cut through the roof, and having twisted their bed-clothes together, in the manner of a ship's cable, to the extent of about 15 fathom [90 feet], would in all probability have effected their escape, had not the sentinel at the back of the Tolbooth discovered them, who giving the alarm, they were properly secured and measures taken to prevent attempts of the like nature in future.

(*Edinburgh Evening Courant*, 12 May 1788)

Ainslie now agreed to turn King's Evidence which gave the prosecution the corroborative evidence that they needed to secure a conviction against Smith and the fugitive Brodie.

Deacon Brodie, having given Williamson the slip, might have got clean away but his luck ran out. In June of that year, a Mr and Mrs Geddes of West Calder boarded a coastal vessel, the *Endeavour*, to sail back to Leith. They had been visiting relatives in London. As the ship was casting off, the captain was hailed by a rowing boat which drew up alongside. An old man muffled in a greatcoat was helped on board. He introduced himself as 'Mr John Dixon'. He presented papers to the captain instructing him to divert to Flushing before proceeding to Leith. Mr Dixon was of course Deacon Brodie in disguise. When he learnt that his fellow passengers were returning to Edinburgh he asked if they could take three letters for him. In the morning in Flushing, the letters were handed over to Mr and Mrs Geddes by Brodie. One of the letters was addressed to Brodie's brother-in-law Matthew Sheriff, another to his friend Michael Henderson while the third was addressed to his mistress Jean Watt. When Mr and Mrs Geddes reached Edinburgh, all the talk was about the forthcoming trial of George Smith and the missing Deacon Brodie.

For three weeks Mr and Mrs Geddes deliberated as to what to do with the letters. They then handed them over to the authorities. The letters were opened and in them Brodie revealed his intention to travel to Amsterdam and there to take ship for New York. He asked that his tools be sent to him in Amsterdam so that he could start a new life in the United States. The hunt was on again.

Readers of the *Courant* must have been astonished to read on 3 July that:

We are informed from good authority, that William Brodie (accused of shop-breaking etc) who absconded from this city about four months ago, has been apprehended in Holland, and is now imprisoned in the Stadhouse at Amsterdam. He is to be delivered up, we learn to the justice of his country and an Excise yacht is immediately to be despatched from Leith for the purpose of bringing him over.

The trial at the High Court in Edinburgh was set for 27 August 1788. Many had queued for hours to get a seat in the packed courtroom. Brodie and Smith were brought in chains from the Tolbooth in Sedan chairs. The trial before Lord Braxfield, the Lord Justice Clerk, commenced at 9.00am. Incredibly the practice then for Scottish trials was that the trial would continue without stopping until a final verdict had been reached. In this trial, Lord Braxfield did not commence his summing-up to the jury until 4.30am and the jury was not sent out to consider their verdict until 6.00am!

Brodie was defended by Henry Erskine, the brilliant Dean of the Faculty of Advocates while Smith was defended by a young, inexperienced advocate John Clerk. The prosecution was led by the Lord Advocate, Ilay Campbell. In total forty-two witnesses were called. Most of the prosecution evidence was circumstantial. For example Robert Smith, Brodie's foreman, confirmed that: 'He had often seen his master in company with Smith and Ainslie.'

Seria mixta jocis

Henry Erskine, Brodie's Defence Counsel.

The damning evidence came from John Brown. Henry Erskine tried to have Brown's evidence discounted, arguing that as a convicted criminal his testimony was worthless but Lord Braxfield over-ruled him pointing out that an amnesty had been granted. For Brodie, Erskine claimed that the defendant had fled Edinburgh because he had been accused of playing with loaded dice. In addition he called on Jean Watt, Brodie's mistress to give him an alibi. Jean Watt swore that:

> On Wednesday the 5th of March last, he [Brodie] came to her house at eight o'clock at night, just as the bell was

Kay's drawing of the trial of Brodie and Smith with the prisoners at the bar.

ringing: that he stayed there all night, and he was not out from the time he came in till near nine o'clock the next morning: that they went early to bed about ten o'clock, as Mr. Brodie complained of being unwell.

This alibi was then confirmed by Jean Watt's servant, Peggy Giles. When it came to the closing speeches by the counsel, Ilay Campbell, briefly summarised the evidence against both defendants. When Smith's counsel John Clerk challenged Lord Braxfield's impartiality in his handling of the case he was firmly told by the judge: 'You are talking nonsense.' Henry Erskine then spoke for over two hours without notes trying to convince the jury of Brodie's innocence. It was now 4.30 in the morning. Lord Braxfield then began his summing-up. He did his best to convince the jury of the guilt of the two prisoners:

Mr Brodie's father, whom I knew, was a very respectable man, and that the son of such a man – himself too, educated to a respectable profession and who had long lived with reputation in it – should be arraigned at this bar for a crime so detestable, is what must affect us all, gentlemen, with sensations of horror ... I can have no doubt in my own mind that Mr Brodie was present at the breaking into the Excise

Office, and as to the other man, Smith, as I have already said, there can be still less doubt about him. If you are the same opinion, gentlemen, you will return a verdict against both prisoners . . .

The jury were sent out and asked to deliver their verdict by 1.00pm that afternoon. The jury unanimously found both men guilty and Lord Braxfield then sentenced them to death by hanging. Their execution was set for 1 October. The prisoners were taken back to the Tolbooth. Brodie, though having been found guilty, was not abandoned by his friends. An appeal was sent to Henry Dundas, a leading Scottish politician and a close friend of William Pitt, the Prime Minister. The appeal argued that the sentence of death was too harsh and that instead, Brodie should be sentenced to a period of transportation. This appeal was rejected and Brodie calmly prepared himself for his execution.

Within three days of the verdicts William Creech was advertising his account of the trial. Creech himself was a member of the jury that had found Brodie guilty. He could well have been taking notes as the trial progressed. However, he would almost certainly have employed several scribes to take down the proceedings in a form of shorthand which would then be collated and edited for inclusion in the book.

While awaiting his execution, Deacon Brodie was visited by several friends. The only time he showed any emotion was when he was visited by his favourite daughter.

He appeared to have no hopes of a pardon, and expressed himself satisfied at the exertions made by his friends on his behalf. On the Friday before his execution, he was visited by his daughter, a fine girl of about ten years of age; and here nature and the feelings of a father were superior to every other consideration, and the falling tear, which he endeavoured to suppress, gave strong proofs of his sensibility – he embraced her with emotion, and blessed her with the warmest affection.

Brodie was also visited in the condemned cell by John Kay, who had been commissioned by William Creech to draw a portrait of Brodie

In a few Days will be Publifhed,
BY WILLIAM CREECH,

A Full Account of the Trial

OF

WILLIAM BRODIE & GEORGE SMITH,

Before the High Court of Jufticiary, on the 27th
and 28th of Auguft 1788 ;

WITH

The Pleadings of the Counfel—the Opinions of the Court
on the contended Points—and the whole Evidence led
before the Jury.

" *Read this, and tremble! ye who 'fcape the Laws.*"
POPE.

The advert in the *Courant* for Creech's account of the trial.

(see page 174) for inclusion in the forthcoming book. On the table next to Brodie, Kay has drawn items that contributed to Brodie's downfall – cards, dice, false keys, ink, quill pens and paper.

1 October 1788 was to be the day of execution. It is reckoned that some 40,000 people packed into the High Street to witness the execution of Brodie and Smith. One of the legends associated with the execution is that Brodie himself had designed the new scaffold with its drop erected on the west gable end of the Tolbooth. This had replaced the old arrangement in the Grassmarket where the condemned person was forced to climb a ladder before being 'cast off'. Death could sometimes take several minutes and friends and relatives in the crowd might try to pull the legs of the sufferer to hasten death. Certainly the new scaffold had been built shortly before 1788 and Brodie may well have had a hand in its construction.

The *Courant* gives us what clearly is an eyewitness account of what transpired that October morning. While a penitent Smith ascended the scaffold in the traditional white linen, Brodie, showman to the last, defied convention and dressed in his fashionable black suit with 'his hair dressed and powdered':

Having put on white night caps [another convention],
Brodie pointed to Smith to ascend the steps that led to the

Mʳ BRODIE

ABOVE. The Execution of Brodie and Smith drawn by John Kay, 1788. (This illustration does not appear in the published *Kay's Portraits* but the style is unmistakably that of John Kay.)

OPPOSITE. Deacon Brodie in the Tolbooth.

drop; and in an easy manner, clapping him on the shoulder said 'George Smith you are first in hand'. Upon this Smith, whose behaviour was highly penitent and resigned slowly ascended the steps, and was immediately followed by Brodie, who mounted with briskness and agility, and examined the dreadful apparatus with attention; and particularly the halter designed for himself. The ropes being too short tied, Brodie stepped down from the platform and entered into conversation with his friends. [An Edinburgh legend suggests that he sang a song from *The Beggar's Opera* to the crowd.]

He then sprang up again, but the rope was still too short; and he once more descended to the platform showing some impatience. [This might well suggest that the authorities were unfamiliar with the operation of the new scaffold?] During this dreadful interval Smith remained on the drop with great composure and placidness. Brodie having ascended a third time, and the rope being at last properly adjusted, he deliberately untied his neckcloth, buttoned up his waistcoat and coat, and helped the executioner to fix the rope. [Another Edinburgh legend is that Brodie had made an arrangement with the executioner to cheat the rope by wearing a steel collar or of having had a tube inserted in his throat. Given that he took off his neckcloth, this seems highly unlikely.]

He then took a friend by the hand, bade him farewell and requested that he would acquaint the world that he was still the same and that he died like a man. He then pulled the nightcap over his face, and placed himself in an attitude expressive of firmness and resolution. Smith, who during all this time had been in fervent devotion, let fall a handkerchief as a signal, and a few minutes before three they were launched into eternity. Brodie on the scaffold neither confessed nor denied his being guilty. Smith, with great fervency, confessed in prayer his being guilty and the justice of his sentence; and showed in all his conduct the proper expression of penitence, humility and faith. This execution was conducted with more than usual solemnity; and the great bell tolled during the ceremony, which had an awful and solemn effect. The crowd of spectators was immense.

There was certainly a degree of sympathy for Brodie. The sentence seems to have been particularly harsh. Brodie himself had pleaded that it be commuted to transportation. However, it may be the case that while the Edinburgh establishment was prepared to tolerate drunkenness, gambling, the keeping of mistresses and frequenting with prostitutes, keeping company with known thieves and engaging in housebreaking and robbing shops was absolutely beyond the pale. Brodie had crossed a line and his crimes were regarded with fear and loathing by his fellow-citizens who condemned him to death. The *Courant* published a form of obituary for Deacon William Brodie and there is more than a hint of both regret and respect for him to be found:

OPPOSITE. George Smith at the bar.

Kay del et sculp 1788

SMITH at the Bar

Thus ended the life of William Brodie, whose conduct, when we consider his situation in life, is equally singular and contradictory. By the low and vicious connections he formed, he had everything to lose – he could gain little even if successful, for, the moment he embarked on the enterprises of his desperate associates, his property, his life was at their mercy. Indeed, his crimes appeared to be rather the result of infatuation rather than depravity, and he seemed to be more attracted by the dexterity of thieving than the profit arising from it . . . Those who know him best agree that his disposition was friendly and generous and that he had infinitely more of the dupe than the knave in his composition; and was indeed admirably fitted for designing and wicked men to work upon . . . The feeling mind would here suggest, to bury with his bones his crimes, his follies and his errors; and whilst we profit by his example, we cannot but lament how improperly those abilities were applied and which might have done honour to himself and his family. His untimely fate claims the tribute of a tear; for those who possess fortitude, courage, benevolence and humanity, claim our admiration; such was William Brodie.

Brodie was gone but of course he became the inspiration for Edinburgh author Robert Louis Stevenson's *Dr. Jekyll and Mr. Hyde*, published in 1886 – the dark tale of a good man by day and a monster at night.

CHAPTER 15

The Trial of
Thomas Muir

By the 1790s, John Kay's reputation as a caricaturist had been well established. As mentioned in chapter 14, William Creech employed Kay to draw and engrave pictures of William Brodie and George Smith for his book of Brodie's trial. As we know, Creech had gone out of his way to draw his readers' attention to the talents of Kay.

In addition to his normal repertoire of subjects, Kay now returned to the High Court and provided illustrations of several notable trials. He was clearly regarded as 'the court artist' of his day. Some of these prints have survived. These include the trials of James McKean convicted of murder in 1796 and Andrew McKinley tried for administering 'unlawful oaths' in 1817. This trial took place against the backdrop of considerable radical unrest, particularly in the West of Scotland, brought about by extreme poverty caused by the economic depression following the conclusion of the Napoleonic Wars in 1815.

There had been a series of strikes and demonstrations that had caused considerable alarm to the authorities. McKinlay, along with twenty-five others, was brought from Glasgow to Edinburgh charged with the serious crime of sedition. The prosecution case rested largely on the evidence of a weaver John Campbell who was then being held as a prisoner in Edinburgh Castle. Under questioning at the trial of McKinley, Campbell admitted that he had agreed to give evidence only on condition that he, his wife and family being helped to leave the country for their own safety. His evidence was ruled as inadmissible and as a result, the prosecution

Thomas White. Midshipman at the Bar
of the high Court of Justiciary for
the Murder of William Jones Seaman
on the Shore of Leith. on the 15ᵗʰ of June 1814.—

Midshipman Thomas White at the bar.

case was severely weakened. The jury found the charge against McKinley to be 'Not Proven'.

The portrait above shows Midshipman Thomas White on trial for the murder of a fellow-seaman, William Jones, in June 1814. Both men had been ashore drinking and Jones had disobeyed an order from White to return to their ship. White had then drawn his cutlass and cut Jones down. White was found guilty of the crime but was spared the death sentence because of his previous good character. He was sentenced instead to fourteen years' transportation to Australia.

The portrait opposite of a man in military uniform is of Professor John Gregory, Head of the School of Medicine at Edinburgh University. Indeed of the 329 plates published in *Kay's Portraits*, no fewer than 51 depict men in some form of military or naval uniform. We should not be too surprised by this when we consider that for some 20 years of Kay's career as an artist, Britain was at war with France. This was a conflict on an unprecedented scale. As well as fighting on Continental Europe and on the high seas, British forces were engaged at some time or another in the West Indies,

Kay's portrait of Professor John Gregory, Head of the School of Medicine,
Edinburgh University.

Canada, Egypt, South Africa, South America, the United States and
India. There was a huge demand for men to join the colours for
service overseas but there was also the urgent question of home
defence to repel the feared French invasion. The response of the
government was to encourage the formation of local militia
regiments. So Gregory is here dressed in the uniform of the Royal
Edinburgh Volunteers formed in 1794.

Kay must have witnessed the Volunteers drilling, and the next illustration shows recruits of all shapes and sizes under the orders of

EDIN. ROYAL VOLUNTEERS.

ABOVE. Military promenade.

OPPOSITE. Edinburgh volunteers.

their commander Colonel Patrick Crichton, an Edinburgh coach-builder and a member of the Town Council. He had served as a regular officer in the British Army during the American War of Independence and survived a shot in the chest incurred when fighting a duel. Kay referred to the regiment in his title as 'the awkward squad'.

The wearing of military uniforms even spread to the world of fashion. Above, Kay has drawn a group walking in the Meadows, a popular area for promenading. Several of the men are in military uniform including one character wearing a veil. This was Captain Hay, 'the Daft Captain' according to Kay, born in Danzig, whose brother was the Prussian consul. He was very eccentric and somewhat short-sighted. He had the habit of peering into women's faces at close quarters. Understandably some women found this behaviour upsetting and chose to draw down their veils on his approach. In retaliation Hay took to wearing his own veil which he lowered when a lady approached him. Two of the ladies shown are clearly in military outfits. These are the Maxwell sisters wearing the uniform of the West Lowland Fencibles of which their father, Sir William Maxwell, was Lieutenant-Colonel.

In August 1793, John Kay was asked to draw Thomas Muir, a Lanarkshire lawyer, who was to go on trial for sedition at the High Court in Edinburgh. This trial was to cause a sensation.

The storming of the Bastille in Paris on 14 July 1789, and the start of the French Revolution, had been enthusiastically welcomed. It seemed that the downfall of the hated 'ancien regime' would usher in a form of constitutional monarchy modelled on that in Great Britain.

> But Europe at that time was thrilled with joy
> France standing on the top of golden hours,
> And human nature seeming born again . . .
> Bliss was it in that dawn to be alive
> But to be young was very heaven!
>
> (William Wordsworth, *The Prelude*)

However, this enthusiasm quickly turned to horror when the revolution descended into bloodthirsty violence with mass executions of political opponents, wealthy landowners and members of the nobility. Many in Britain feared that the revolution would spread across the Channel with dreadful consequences for the British ruling class and the monarchy. Parliament rushed through draconian laws designed to suppress any attempts to challenge the established political control. Habeus Corpus was suspended, several radicals were arrested and a network of spies and informers was put in place. It became dangerous for groups of people to meet to protest or even to discuss political affairs such as an extension of the franchise.

An idea of just how unrepresentative Scottish politics were can be gauged by the fact that only twenty-five people elected Edinburgh's one MP and in the election of 1790, Henry Dundas, Viscount Melville, controlled thirty-three of the forty-five Scottish seats. The French Revolution though had acted as a catalyst to demands for reform. The Society of Friends of the People in Scotland was formed in 1792. The King's birthday on 4 June 1792 was greeted by three days of serious rioting in Edinburgh. Two of the rioters were charged with sedition

and put on trial. Both were sentenced to fourteen years' transportation. One of them, Alex Lockie, was defended by Thomas Muir.

Muir had been born on 25 August 1765, the son of a wealthy Glasgow merchant. Throughout his life, Muir held deeply religious views and was an elder of the Church of Scotland. He had intended to train for the ministry but had switched courses and studied Law at Glasgow University. However, while a student, he showed his determination to contest a cause where he saw the abuse of power. With others, Muir challenged the university authorities and as a consequence was banned from attending further lectures. Muir withdrew from Glasgow and enrolled at Edinburgh University where he completed his legal studies. He went into practise and was successful in several high-profile cases which brought him to the attention of senior legal figures in Scotland, including Lord Braxfield, the Lord Justice Clerk, Scotland's senior judge, and Robert Dundas, the Lord Advocate. Both of these men would play a critical role in Muir's subsequent trial.

Muir was very influenced by the writings of the radical Thomas Paine, author of the influential *Rights of Man*, and was inspired by the events of the French Revolution. He organised a debating club which styled itself 'The Friends of the People' and campaigned for an extension of the franchise. Muir became the Vice-President of the Scottish Society of the Friends of the People and entered into correspondence with the United Irishmen campaigning for Irish independence. Inevitably this provoked the hostility of the political establishment. Henry Erskine, the Dean of the Faculty of Advocates, led a campaign that saw Muir being expelled from the Faculty.

More 'radical trials' followed. In 1794 Robert Watt was found guilty of treason and hanged at the Tolbooth. Several of Muir's radical friends were arrested and charged with sedition. In January 1793 Muir himself was arrested by Mr Williamson, the King's Messenger (of Deacon Brodie fame) on his way to Edinburgh to attend the trial of his friend James Tytler who had been charged with sedition for publishing a pamphlet championing the Rights of Man. This was the same James Tytler, the balloonist, whom we met in chapter 12. Tytler fled before his trial could start. He was outlawed. Tytler went first to Dublin and then to the United States of America. Muir meanwhile was interrogated by two sheriffs but vigorously contested the legitimacy of his arrest: 'Such examinations are utterly inconsistent with the rights of British subjects . . . They are instruments of oppression and pregnant with mischief.'

Muir was released on bail and travelled to France in a vain attempt to save the life of Louis XVI. He was arrested by the Revolutionary authorities and so missed his trial date in Edinburgh. As a result he was outlawed and arrested on his return to Scotland in July 1793.

> Mr Muir (late advocate) who was outlawed by the High Court of Justiciary, accused of seditious practices, landed on Tuesday at Port-Patrick from Ireland. He was immediately known and apprehended, brought to Stranraer and lately lodged in jail. It appears from his passports, that he had lately left France, from whence he came to Ireland. He is to be brought immediately to Edinburgh.
>
> (*Edinburgh Evening Courant*, 3 August 1793)

> Thursday August 5th Mr. Muir was brought to town from Stranraer by Mr. Williamson, messenger, under a judiciary warrant, and lodged in the tollbooth [sic], till liberated in due course of law.
>
> (*Edinburgh Evening Courant*, 7 August 1793)

OPPOSITE. George Williamson, the King's Messenger who arrested Muir.

Thomas Muir's friend and fellow-member of the Society of Friends of the People, William Skirving, was also arrested and brought to Edinburgh. As the *Courant* reported on 10 August:

> On Wednesday afternoon [7 August], William Skirving, Secretary to the Friends of the People was apprehended, brought before the Sheriff, and examined respecting some seditious publications lately circulated in this city. He was yesterday re-examined and again committed to prison till liberated in due course of the law.

Muir was brought before Lord Braxfield to answer the charge and to attempt to obtain bail. The Lord Advocate, Robert Dundas objected. Muir appealed to the bench.

> Mr. Muir being asked if he had anything to say, he bowed and addressed the Court in a short, firm speech, in which he observed that so far from hurting his country, he believed he had done it essential service; that he wished for nothing more than a trial, in which he was persuaded his innocence would appear. Mr. Muir petitioned the Court to be admitted to bail . . . that, in a crowded jail, and in a room open to all sorts of company, he had not an opportunity to prepare his defence . . . he was admitted to bail – the penalty 2000 merks Scots [about £10,000 today].
>
> (*Edinburgh Evening Courant*, 15 August 1793)

Muir's trial commenced in Edinburgh on 30 August 1793 with the notorious Lord Braxfield plus four other judges on the Bench. The courtroom was packed. Henry Erskine, the Dean of the Faculty of Advocates, had offered to defend Muir free of charge but Muir was determined to have his day in court. Perhaps he appreciated that the odds were very heavily stacked against him so saw his trial as an important public platform to speak out against what he saw as the injustices of the British political system. The charge against Muir was read out. He was

> accused of wickedly and feloniously. . . by means of seditious speeches and harangues a spirit of disloyalty and disaffection

to the King and the established government – of advising and extorting other persons to purchase and peruse seditious and wicked publications and writings (viz Paine's works, a declaration of rights, the *Patriot* etc).

Muir opened his defence with a brief statement to the court. He claimed that:

he had uniformly advised the people to pursue legal and constitutional measures; and that he had also advised them to read all books written upon the great natural question of reform.

Muir then objected to each one of the fifteen jurors chosen to hear the case claiming that:

they were all subscribers to the Goldsmiths' Hall association and offered a reward for discovering those who had circulated what they deemed seditious writings, and they had already prejudged him and were therefore improper persons to pass upon his assize.

The jury comprised Gilbert Innes of Stow; Sir James Fowler of Colinton; Captain John Inglis of Auchindinny; John Wauchope of Edmonstone; John Balfour, younger of Pilrig; Andrew Wauchope; Niddry Marischal; John Trotter of Mortonhall; James Rocheid of Inverleith; John Alves of Dalkeith; William Dalrymple, Merchant; Donald Smith, Banker; James Dickson, Bookseller; Grant Kinnear, Banker; Andrew Fisher, Merchant; and John Horner, Merchant.

Muir was quite right to fear that the hand-picked jury would be hostile to him. Compared to the jury that had convicted Deacon Brodie which had been composed of a mixture of merchants, shopkeepers and fellow-tradesmen, this jury was made up exclusively of landed gentlemen, two wealthy merchants and a banker.

His plea was rejected by Lord Braxfield and proceedings got underway. Much of the prosecution evidence against Muir was centred round a meeting of the Friends of the People held in Kirkintilloch in November 1792. Muir tried hard to convince the Court that several of the prosecution witnesses had been coached in their evidence and as such, they should be disregarded as hostile witnesses. He claimed that he could prove that Andrew Johnstone, a bleacher, had 'said he would do everything in his power to have him [Muir] hanged'. Muir's objections were over-ruled. He was, however, successful in having the evidence of Reverend Mr James Lapsie, Minister of Campsie, disregarded for 'having been present at the examination of other prosecution witnesses and even putting questions to some of them'.

After the conclusion of the trial, Kay drew a very unflattering portrait of Lapslie and branded him 'Pension Hunter'. The accompanying notes to the portrait quoted a contemporary rhyme criticising the minister:

> My name is Jamie Lapslie
> I preach and I pray
> And as an informer
> Expect a good fee

Matters became particularly heated when Muir objected to the evidence of the principal prosecution witness, Ann Fisher, formerly a servant in the home of his father. She swore that she had witnessed Muir sending copies of Paine's works to be printed and then distributing copies. Muir challenged her evidence claiming that it was a fabrication. The *Courant* reported that:

> He [Muir] said that the conduct of the Lord Advocate was in every way reprehensible. He has put a variety of questions to witnesses with regard to crimes of which I am not accused. The indictment charges me with making seditious speeches at Kirkintilloch and at Campsie, vilifying the Constitution and the King. And inflaming the minds of people to rebellion. It charges me with distribution of seditious books – and it specifies that I gave away Mr. Paine's works ... the indictment charges nothing more. There is not a word within its four corners which points out to me the charge of speaking disrespectfully of Courts of Justice or 'tending' in any manner to excite the people against the administration of the law. If the

OPPOSITE. Kay's portrait of Rev. James Lapslie.

PENSION HUNTER

Public Prosecutor had evidence that I was guilty of a crime of this nature he ought to have made it an article of association and then I would have defended myself in the best way that I could. But to attempt to steal it in as evidence in this way to prove a crime which he durst not openly libel because he knew it would not be supported, deserves the severest reprobation. I know the tendency of this little art. This witness – this domestic and well-tutored spy, is brought to prove words which may irritate the minds of your lordships against me. Yes this is the artifice – this is the object – but my Lords I contend upon the great principles of natural justice – upon the established law of this country, that no person can be charged with a crime of which he has not been accused.

Muir's complaints were contemptuously dismissed by Lord Braxfield. The judge added that 'he had never heard a more distinct and accurate witness [Ann Fisher] in his life.' His colleagues on the bench, Lords Henderland, Swinton, Dunsinnan and Abercrombie, concurred.

In his defence, Muir produced a group of witnesses all of whom attested to the fact that Muir had not encouraged rebellion and had argued for restraint. William Skirving of Strathguddie, who was already under arrest for sedition, stated that Muir had been deputed by the Friends of the People Society in London to travel to France 'in order to see if he could have any influence to prevent the execution of the King'. Skirving continued that '. . . he had been frequently in company with Mr. Muir, both in societies and privately, and never heard him speak against the constitution but the reverse; that his whole conduct was of a contrary tendency, and that he disapproved of Mr. Paine's principles of government'.

Skirving was followed by James Campbell, Writer to the Signet who stated that: 'He never heard Mr. Muir speak against the constitution but had heard him say Paine's works were dangerous for weak minds.'

Other witnesses called by Muir included George Waddel, manufacturer, Glasgow; Daniel McArthur, Master of the Grammar School, Glasgow; and John Russell, merchant, also of Glasgow. Russell was asked by Dundas what he had been told to say. Russell answered 'the truth'. When asked who had told him to say this, the

Kay's portrait of Thomas Paine.

witness replied 'that as everybody believed in this he couldn't answer specifically.' He was then accused of being 'guilty of concealing the truth on oath' and was sentenced to three weeks in the Tolbooth! Another witness for the defence, the Reverend Mr Dunn of Kirkintilloch was also sent to the Tolbooth for three months for preaching what was considered to be a radical sermon.

By now it was past 10.00pm. The Lord Advocate's summing-up was very brief and referred the jury members to Muir's avowed support for parliamentary reform which Dundas presented as a threat to the British constitution and a step towards revolution. Muir spoke for over two hours to an increasingly impatient jury, who clearly had already reached a decision regarding his guilt. Muir famously concluded his defence by stating that: 'I have devoted myself to the cause of The People. It is a good cause – it shall ultimately prevail – it shall finally triumph.' When Muir at last sat down, the courtroom erupted with cheering and loud applause. Lord Braxfield's summing-up was brutal.

> There was a spirit of sedition and revolt going abroad which rendered every good subject seriously uneasy. And I leave it to you to judge whether it was perfectly innocent or not in Mr. Muir at such time going among ignorant country people and among the lower classes of people . . . inducing them to believe that a reform was absolutely necessary to preserve their safety and their liberty which til then they had never suspected to be in danger.

The court rose at 2.00am on 31 August for the jury to consider its verdict. At 12 noon the jury delivered a unanimous verdict of guilty. Muir was sentenced to transportation to Botany Bay for fourteen years.

Amongst the packed audience in the courtroom there must have been a number of short-hand writers taking down as best they could the words of Thomas Muir and Robert Dundas; the evidence presented by the various witnesses and the pronouncements of Lord Braxfield. There was a rush to publish accounts of the trial. As early as 2 September, just two days after the conclusion of the trial, the *Courant* carried four separate advertisements for forthcoming books on the trial of Thomas Muir.

> In the press and speedily will be published *An Account of the Trial of Thomas Muir.*

The first to be published was that by James Simpson which went on sale on Thursday 5 September 1793 at a price of 1/6d (7.5p) William Creech's account was published on 7 September and James Robertson's on Thursday 12 September. James Robertson's advert claimed:

> The Public may rely on the Authenticity of this Account as the evidence was taken down accurately in the Court and

MR MUIR'S TRIAL.

On Saturday will be Publifhed,

By A. SCOTT, Gazetteer Office, South Bridge-ftreet, Edinburgh—and fold by the Bookfellers of London, Glafgow,
Aberdeen, Perth, Dundee, &c.

T H E

TRIAL OF THOMAS MUIR, ESQ.
YOUNGER OF HUNTERSHILL,

Before the High Court of Jufticiary, upon Friday and
Saturday, the 30th and 31ft Auguft 1793.

This very momentous and interefting Trial, which occupied the fpace of Eighteen Hours, was accurately taken down
by an eminent Short-hand Writer. The Publifher will be
alfo affifted with the Notes of feveral Gentlemen prefent.—
The authenticity of this Edition may therefore be depended
upon.

To which will be prefixed, a STRIKING LIKENESS of
Mr MUIR, to be engraved by Mr Kay.

☞ The Profits to be appropriated to any Charitable Purpofe
Mr Muir may direct.

An advert from *The Edinburgh Evening Courant* for one of the first books
published on the trial of Thomas Muir.

Mr. Muir has taken the trouble (at the publisher's solicita-
tion) to revise the Notes which were taken of his SPEECH to
the jury.

A further book was published by A. Scott, Gazetteer Office, South
Bridge Street:

This very momentous and interesting Trial which occupied
the span of Eighteen Hours, was accurately taken down by
an eminent short-hand writer. The publication will also be
assisted with the notes of several gentlemen present. The
authenticity of this edition may therefore be depended
upon. To which will be prefaced a STRIKING LIKENESS of
Mr. Muir to be engraved by Mr. Kay. The profits to be appropriated to any Charitable Purpose Mr. Muir may direct.

I.Kay 1793

Illustrious Martyr in the glorious cause
Of truth, of freedom, and of equal laws.

What is particularly interesting in this portrait is that Kay has made his own political sympathies crystal-clear: 'Illustrious Martyr in the glorious cause. Of truth, of freedom and of equal laws.' Given the establishment's hostility to anything that hinted at sedition, this was a very brave statement for Kay to make.

Along with Muir, a group of other so-called 'radicals' were shortly to go on trial. These included the Reverend Thomas Palmer, William Skirving, Maurice Margarot and Joseph Gerrald. Lord Braxfield was again the senior judge at these trials. He proved himself to be extremely hostile to the accused and did his best to influence the jury. Braxfield was later accused of commenting to a juryman that: 'They would a' be the muckle the better o' being hanged.' The accused, however, were quite prepared to stand up to Braxfield. Having been threatened by Lord Braxfield, William Skirving replied: 'It is altogether unavailing for your lordship to menace me; for I have long learned to fear not the face of man.' While Margarot, who also defended himself, made fun of Lord Braxfield's broad Scottish accent. In reply to Braxfield's query 'Hae ye ony counsel, man?' Margarot replied: 'No, I only want an interpreter to make me understand what your lordship says.' Gerrald, who also defended himself, pointed out that 'Christianity was an innovation and that all great men had been reformers, even our Saviour himself.' Braxfield leaned over the bench and with a wicked grin replied: 'Aye, and muckle he made o' that, he was hangit!'

Not surprisingly, all the accused were found guilty and sentenced to long terms of transportation to Australia: Margarot, Gerrald and Skirving to fourteen years, while Thomas Palmer, who had already been convicted, had been sentenced to seven years. The prisoners were taken in chains on board the Excise yacht the *Royal George* anchored in Leith and carried to London. They were then confined in one of the notorious prison hulks awaiting transportation to Botany Bay. Attempts were made in Parliament to have their sentences reviewed but on the morning of 24 May, they were abruptly shipped out for the new penal colony (Botany Bay was only established in 1788), on board the *Surprise*, arriving in Australia on 24 October 1794.

OPPOSITE. Kay's portrait of Thomas Muir.

Many were shocked by this brutal treatment. In a poem not published until after his death, Robert Burns wrote:

> The shrinking Bard down the alley skulks,
>   And dreads a meeting worse than Woolwich hulks,
> Though here, his heresies in Church and state
>   Might well award him Muir and Palmer's fate.
>
>   (From Robert Burns, 'Esopus to Maria')

Clearly, while supporting the convicted men, Burns was fearful for his own position. He had deliberately sent the manuscript for 'Scots Wha Hae' for publication to George Thomson on 30 August 1793 – the date set for the start of the trial of Muir. In the note that accompanied the manuscript, Burns had referred to: 'that glorious struggle for Freedom, associated with the glowing ideas of some other struggles of the same nature, not quite so ancient!' Although the words of the stirring anthem were meant to refer to the speech of Robert Bruce before the 1314 Battle of Bannockburn, they clearly had a very contemporary ring to them:

> By oppressions woes and pains,
> By your sons in servile chains,
> We will drain your dearest veins,
> But they shall be free!
> Lay the proud usurpers low!
> Tyrants fall in every foe!
> Liberty's in every blow! –
> Let us do, or die!

The prisoners survived the long voyage. Conditions in the penal colony were not too harsh. The convicted men were allocated their own huts and were able to purchase small tracts of land for farming. A daring plan to rescue Muir was carried out in 1796 by an American ship, the *Otter*. A Royal Naval blockade prevented him from being landed in the USA and Muir actually spent some time imprisoned in Havana. Eventually he was transferred to a Spanish ship, the *Ninfa*, bound for Cadiz, and set sail early in 1797. Unfortunately this ship was intercepted by British warships off the coast of Spain on 26 April and severely damaged. Muir himself was badly

The Memorial Obelisk, known as 'The Martyrs' Monument', in the Calton Burial Ground erected in 1844 by the 'Friends of Parliamentary Reform in England and Scotland'.

wounded, a piece of shrapnel shattering his left cheekbone and permanently damaging his sight. He was taken ashore and promptly imprisoned by the Spanish authorities. The French government, however, secured his release. He arrived in France in 1797 and was hailed as a hero of the French Revolution. Sadly he never recovered from his wounds and died at Chantilly in September 1799.

Of the other 'Scottish Martyrs' as they were called, only Margarot survived and returned to Scotland. Both Gerrald and Skirving died in Botany Bay. Palmer served his time but died at Guam on his way home. Their fate aroused much public sympathy and an obelisk known as the 'Martyrs' Monument' was erected to their memory in Edinburgh's Calton Burial Ground in 1844. The monument is inscribed with the names of the five men together with Muir's famous declaration from the dock:

> I have devoted myself to the cause of The People. It is a good cause – it shall ultimately prevail

and William Skirving's words on conviction:

> I know that what has been done these two days will be Re-Judged.

CHAPTER 16

'Carle, Now the King's Come'

By the summer of 1822, John Kay had reached the advanced age of 80. Almost certainly failing eyesight and arthritic fingers had forced him to give up his work as a caricaturist and engraver. Sadly it meant that Kay was unable to capture anything of the celebrated visit of George IV in the August of that year. However, living as he was in nearby Parliament Close and with windows looking out onto the thoroughfare, it is reasonable to assume that Kay would witness some of the events of the momentous days when George IV came to Edinburgh.

At a dinner in London in 1815, Walter Scott had persuaded George, who was then Prince Regent, that he was as much a Stuart as Bonnie Prince Charlie had been. He should come to his royal capital of the ancient kingdom of his ancestors. George was flattered by the suggestion and agreed in principle that the proposed visit should go ahead once he had succeeded his father, the ailing George III. This event though did not happen until 1820. In the meantime, George gave permission for Sir Walter Scott to search for the lost Scottish regalia in Edinburgh Castle.

In 1707 following the Act of Union, the ancient regalia of Scotland had been surrendered by William, 9th Earl Marischal, to the custody of the Earl of Glasgow, Treasurer-Deputy of Scotland. The Scottish Crown, Sword of State and Sceptre were then placed in a wooden chest in the old Crown Room of Edinburgh Castle. The room was locked and the Regalia were quietly forgotten. On 5 November 1794, during a search for some lost Parliamentary papers,

'The Honours of Scotland'. The discovery of the Scottish Regalia (Sir David
Wilkie). Sir Walter Scott is standing on the right holding the sheet.

the room was broken open by the Castle's Governor, Lieutenant-
General Drummond. The chest was discovered and shaken but not
opened. The Governor thought that it sounded empty. Rumours
swept the country that the regalia were lost, stolen or had been taken
secretly to London where they were now on display in the Tower.

In 1817 the Prince Regent issued a warrant authorising the room
to be searched again and the chest to be opened. With Sir Walter
Scott in attendance, the room was searched. No keys had been
found so the king's locksmith was present to force open the chest.
It was a very emotional moment when the lid was pushed open.
Scott described the scene:

> The joy was therefore extreme when, the ponderous lid
> having been forced open ... the regalia were discovered lying
> at the bottom covered with linen cloths, exactly as they had
> been left in 1707.

Thousands had gathered around the Castle waiting for news. A flag was raised on the battlements to show that the mission to find the regalia had been successful. There was great rejoicing and thousands took to the streets to celebrate.

In 1820, old George III died. He had been on the throne since 1760. The new king, George IV, was deeply unpopular. He was now aged fifty-six. The excesses of his private life were well-known. Many years of over-indulgence had taken its toll. George was given to heavy drinking and was grossly overweight. In 1797 he had tipped the scales at 17.5 stones and boasted a waist measurement of 51 inches. His scandalous private life was keeping the gossip-mongers happy. Following a string of affairs he had married his mistress, the twice-widowed Maria Fitzherbert, on 15 December 1785. This marriage outraged his father and was declared null and void as George had failed to seek permission for the union. To make matters worse, Mrs Fitzherbert was a Roman Catholic. The need for an heir required another marriage. So, although George continued his relationship with Mrs Fitzherbert, he married his cousin Caroline, Countess of Brunswick, on 8 April 1795. He soon became disgusted with her and in 1799 she was banished from the Court. Caroline was effectively confined to Montague House, home of the Earl of Sandwich. There she entertained a string of lovers including George Canning and Sir Sidney Smith and gave birth to a son. George meantime, while continuing his relationship with Mrs Fitzherbert, took on a new mistress, Frances Villiers, Countess of Jersey.

In 1814, Caroline was ordered out of the country. She travelled around the Continent attracting the attention of yet more lovers. George failed in his legal attempt to have her stripped of her title. However, the death of her father-in-law George III in 1820 brought Caroline home for the Coronation. Her return was greeted enthusiastically by the London mob, who had taken her to their hearts, but not by her husband, now George IV. Caroline was actually locked out of the Coronation Service held at Westminster on 21 July 1821. She retired, cheered by the mob. Within three weeks, however, she was dead. It was widely rumoured that she had been poisoned. There was no autopsy so the cause of her death was never formally established. George was deeply unpopular and was probably only too pleased to escape from London. Nevertheless he was now the King and the King was coming to Edinburgh.

The intended visit in August was announced in a letter to the

A contemporary cartoon of George IV.

Lord Provost which was not received until July. There was wide-spread panic at the short notice as this was to be the first visit by a reigning monarch since the short stay of the fugitive Charles II in 1650. Sir Walter Scott was put in charge of the arrangements. He set up a committee – Colonel David Stewart of Garth, James Skene of Rubislaw, William Murray, manager of the Theatre Royal, and Alexander Keith of Ravelston, the Knight Marischal of Scotland. This was to be a celebration of Scotland and in particular the Highlands of Scotland. Walter Scott rushed out an anonymous guide to his fellow-Scots on the etiquette to be observed during the forthcoming Royal visit. The *Hints addressed to the inhabitants of Edinburgh and others in prospect of His Majesty's Visit by an old citizen* sold out at 1/- (5p) a copy. Advice was given as to dress and behaviour. Gentlemen were to wear uniform if entitled to it; 'blue coats, white waistcoat and white or nankeen trousers with a low-browed hat with a saltire or heather attached'. However, quite clearly the expectation was that tartan was to be the order of the day. Those attending the planned Balls for the King were advised that: 'No gentleman is to be allowed to appear in anything but the ancient Highland costume.'

In addition, those wearing tartan had to be properly armed with a pair of pistols, a broadsword and a dirk. It is worth remembering that it was only in 1782, that the post-Culloden proscription on the wearing of tartan was lifted.

When would the King come? As late as 22 July 1822, Robert Peel, the Home Secretary, wrote to Lord Liverpool 'Has the King made up his mind with respect to Scotland?' Word reached Scott that the King intended to sail from Greenwich on 10 August arriving at Leith on the 14th. An army of workmen was engaged to clean the streets and to knock down ruinous buildings. These included the old Butter Tron at the foot of the Castlehill. Water and gas were piped into Holyrood Palace, though it was agreed that the King and his entourage were to stay at the splendid Dalkeith Palace, home to the sixteen-year-old 5th Duke of Buccleuch. The approach road to Dalkeith Palace was rerouted and a special laundry and dairy were hurriedly constructed. Billets had to be found for the hundreds of soldiers who were to be drafted into the town. Four Bow Street Runners were sent to Edinburgh to deal with the flood of London pickpockets expected to come north with the King. The King's enormous royal household was brought by sea. *The City of Edinburgh* steam packet brought one hundred cases of plate and the King's Throne to Leith from where it was taken by cart to Dalkeith Palace. In anticipation six cannon were hauled to the top of the Bass Rock in the Firth of Forth and a forty-five foot flagpole was erected to salute the arrival of the royal visitor. A huge bonfire was built on the top of Arthur's Seat. In addition, Edinburgh braced itself for the influx of thousands of visitors anxious to be part of the celebrations. The *Glasgow Herald* reported that:

> Glasgow, as far as we can see, will be almost deserted on the occasion – every vehicle of conveyance is fully employed and

engaged for the coming days. Extra boats on the canal are insufficient for the number of passengers. Where the moving mass from all corners of the land are to stow themselves when in Edinburgh, we know not. Many, we understand, are provided with or are providing themselves with tents and intend to bivouac in the fields.

Scott was bombarded with letters and petitions from Scotland's noble families claiming ancient titles and privileges that would put them centre-stage during the visit. For example the 18th Earl of Errol claimed to be the hereditary Lord High Constable of Scotland with the right to carry the Sword of State. Lord Francis Stafford, son of the Countess of Sutherland, hugely unpopular for clearing her estates to replace her tenants with sheep, was to carry the Sceptre. The Sutherland clansmen who accompanied their Chief had to be kitted out in Black Watch tartan borrowed from Stirling Castle. Meanwhile a veritable army of unemployed tailors was busily making tartan outfits for those hoping to be part of the festivities.

As well as co-ordinating all the arrangements for the visit, Scott somehow found time to write a song of celebration 'Carle, Now The King's Come'. The song had thirty-seven verses. Here is one of them:

> The news has flown frae mouth to mouth,
> The North for ance has bang'd the South;   [beaten]
> The de'il a Scotsman's die o' drouth,   [thirst]
> Carle, now the King's come!

> *Chorus:*
> Carle, now the King's come!
> Carle, now the King's come!
> Thou shalt dance, and I will sing,
> Carle, now the King's come!

Sir Thomas Mash, Controller of Accounts in the Lord Chamberlain's office, arrived in Edinburgh to take control. Scott would not give way.

> When his Majesty comes amongst us, he comes to his ancient kingdom of Scotland and must be received

according to ancient usages. If you persist in bringing in English customs we turn about, one and all, and leave you. You take the responsibility on yourself.

Mash backed down. It was to be Scott's show.

Incredibly Scott found time to metamorphose the Company of Archers, a social club for wealthy gentlemen formed at the end of the 17th century, into the ancient Royal Bodyguard of Scotland. A new uniform was created and officers appointed under the command of the 4th Earl of Hopetoun, a veteran of the Napoleonic wars.

On 22 July, Scott wrote a personal letter to every Highland chief summoning them to Edinburgh: 'The King is coming after all! Arms and men are the best things that we have to show him.' There was a very positive response, given the little time that there was for the clan chiefs to make arrangements. Lt.-Col. Sir Ewan Murray MacGregor, Chief of the Clan Gregor, brought fifty men to Edinburgh. They were fitted out with tartan from a supplier in the North Bridge with their weapons provided by John McLeod of Castle Street. The weapons alone cost £148. The officers were provided with grander costumes supplied by Romanes and Paterson at the Scottish Tartan Warehouse in North Bridge. The four brigades were also supplied with whisky – a gallon a day per brigade of ten men.

There was a tremendous scramble for somewhere to stay. Edinburgh householders made a killing. The Duke of Atholl rented Lady Seaforth's house in Charlotte Square for 100 guineas (£105) for the duration of the visit. Property in Abercromby Place was offered for 130 guineas and in York Place for 70 guineas.

On Monday 12 August, the King's birthday, the Honours of Scotland were moved from the Castle down the Lawnmarket, to Holyrood Palace. Crowds rushed to see the procession. Many clambered onto the half-finished scaffolding on the Castle Esplanade which collapsed. Two were killed and several more seriously injured. It was estimated that some 60,000 visitors had made their way to Edinburgh for the Royal visit.

Gunfire heralded the sighting of the royal fleet in the early

OPPOSITE. Moving the Regalia of Scotland from Edinburgh Castle to Holyrood House on 12 August 1822 before the King's arrival (James Skene, 1822).

afternoon of Wednesday 14 August. Amongst the boats which welcomed the King was the luxury yacht owned by Sir William Curtis, former Lord Mayor of London who had made his fortune from banking and supplying ships' biscuits to the Royal Navy. He was a regular drinking chum of the King's. Thousands flocked to Leith to welcome the King – but it was pouring with rain. Scott boarded the Royal Yacht to greet the King and suggested postponing his landing. George agreed and word was sent ashore that the landing had been put off until the next day to the huge disappointment of the assembled thousands of spectators. However, the enormous bonfire on Arthur's Seat was lit and burned through the night.

Thankfully the next day dawned fair and sunny. The King would land that morning. The escort of Highlanders mustered in Queen Street Gardens. They were joined by Sir Walter Scott dressed in trews as a sore rash prevented him from wearing a kilt. They set off for Leith and were joined by the military, the Officers of State, Yeomen of the Guard and the Royal Company of Archers.

The *Royal George* docked and at mid-day the King was brought ashore in the Royal Barge wearing the uniform of Admiral of the Fleet (see Plate 12). He received a tumultuous welcome. George spent fifteen minutes being introduced to dignitaries. He spotted the 7th Earl of Elgin, who had recently acquired the 'Elgin Marbles' for the British Museum, standing in his uniform of the Royal Company of Archers and went to shake his hand.

There was tremendous excitement as the royal procession proceeded up Leith Walk. Part-way up the King was met by the Lord Provost William Arbuthnot at a specially constructed archway. The procession then proceeded along Picardy Place, York Place then up into St Andrew Square. The carriages then turned left into Princes Street and moved across Regent Bridge (named after George) and along Waterloo Place, down Abbeyhill to Holyrood Palace. When the King saw the crowds on Calton Hill singing the National Anthem, he was overcome with emotion and wept. The procession arrived at Holyrood at 1.40pm. There he received the leading members of the Scottish nobility, the Honours of Scotland and a loyal address from the Lord Provost. At 3.30pm the King was driven to Dalkeith Palace.

The scene was witnessed by the young Jane and Mary Grant,

daughters of John Grant of Rothiemurcas. The two sisters aged
twenty-one and eighteen had travelled with their father for the great
occasion. It took them two days to cover the 150 km from their
family home in Speyside. The girls wrote vivid descriptions of their
experiences in letters to their mother who had had to stay at home
to nurse their sick brother. On the morning of 15 August, the Grants
took their allotted positions in a house in Picardy Place. They shared
the house with sixty other people including the family of James
Loch, the factor of the Duke and Duchess of Sutherland – the man
responsible for the Clearances on the family estates. Jane wrote:

> We were off at ten equipped as yesterday. The servants in full
> dress liveries, the horses decorated with new scarlet cockades
> and cloth padding under the saddles of their bright rubbed
> harness. It was a lovely morning, sun shining splendid; the
> heavens bright and clear; the whole scene gay and smiling
> . . . All the stages and platforms crowded with people; the
> windows of each tall house full to the very top; the Calton
> Hill covered with tents and spectators; the streets crowded
> on every side, and a broad empty space lined with yeomanry
> left in the middle for the coming procession. Even the roofs
> of the houses were covered with people standing upright by
> the chimneys or clinging where they could; the doors and
> steps of the houses all full; boys seated on the tops of the
> lamp posts and hanging up the posts.
>
> The procession was beautiful. I think the King's carriage
> splendid; he was very gracious and each lady in our three
> houses declared he gave her a particular bow . . . I saw him
> take off his hat very gracefully; and everybody said he looked
> quite pleased and delighted; but when he got further
> through the town they complained that he looked fagged
> and did not raise his hat quite so high.

Later that evening she and her family strolled through the New
Town:

> Every street in every corner of the town was literally filled with
> people of every rank; not merely the footways on each side
> but the broad pavement [the street] held a moving mass

A contemporary print making fun of King George's short kilt.

whichever way you went. Most of the houses were simply lighted with candles, some in every pane; others in figures ...

Friday 16 August was a rest day for the King but a night of illuminations, fireworks and cannonades in Edinburgh. On Saturday 17 August a short levee was held at Holyrood Palace. The King was in full Highland costume with flesh-coloured silk tights. in a rather short kilt which prompted one observer, Lady Hamilton-Dalrymple, to remark: 'Since his stay was so short, the more we see of him the better.'

The King was joined by Sir William Curtis, also in full Highland dress. Many of those present strongly disapproved of the King's disreputable friend squeezed into an ill-fitting kilt. George spent only seventy-five minutes being presented to twelve hundred Scottish nobles and lairds – an average of four seconds for each one.

Sunday 18 August was another rest day for the King. This was followed by two further days of presentations at the Palace. On Monday the King had to listen to long addresses from the Church of Scotland, the Scottish Universities, and the Highland Society. Sir John Sinclair of Ulbster presented the King with a copy of his *Statistical Account of Scotland*. Then on the next day 457 ladies were presented to the King. Each received a kiss on the cheek. The levee started at 2.15 and was over by 3.30.

On Wednesday, once again there were no public engagements for the King. He hosted a supper party at Dalkeith attended by a few close associates including Sir Walter Scott. Music was provided by Nathaniel Gow's Celebrated Band. Nathaniel was the son of the famous Scottish fiddler, Neil Gow.

It would be nice to think that old John Kay either witnessed the next day's procession in the High Street or was one the crowd who packed onto the Castle Esplanade to cheer the King's visit to the Castle. The whole of the Royal Mile was lined with temporary stands. The Esplanade stands had been hastily repaired following the accident of 12 August. The rain poured down. The parade was to be led by 'The Tartan Confederacy' – all the assembled clansmen and the Celtic Society. They were joined by the Scottish Officers of State and the Scottish Regalia. The King was in a closed carriage. The procession left Holyrood at 2.00pm. The *Scotsman* reported:

> The High Street presented a most brilliant and spirit-stirring spectacle. The windows and the galleries in front of the houses were filled with the assembled beauty and fashion of Scotland.

Once again thousands turned up to witness the historic event. It was rumoured that people had been prepared to pay as much as £100 (equivalent to about £8,000 today) for a window seat and even more for a box seat on the Castle Esplanade. The King was presented with the keys of the Castle by the Governor. He was then carried up to the Half-Moon Battery to a specially constructed platform erected to take the salute from the cheering crowds. George was overwhelmed by the occasion.

> Good God! What a fine sight! I had no conception there was such a fine scene in the world and to find it in my own dominions and the people are as extraordinary and beautiful as the scene.

King George on the Half-Moon Battery, Edinburgh Castle (James Skene, 1822).

On being advised to step down from his platform because he was now getting wet, George replied: 'Rain? I feel no rain. Never mind. I must cheer the people.' Which he did. George stood for fifteen minutes acknowledging the cheers of the drenched crowds below.

The bad weather continued on the following day. Scott had arranged a Royal Review on Portobello Sands. At the King's request the three thousand volunteer cavalrymen were joined by the Highlanders who were given last-minute drill by Stewart of Gask in Queen Street Gardens. The parade was ready by noon. Fifty thousand spectators had turned up to watch. At 1.15 the King arrived in an open coach. He mounted his horse and rode up and down the lines three times. He forgot to inspect the Highlanders who had been positioned at some distance from the Yeomanry. This omission was conveyed to the King who asked that they join in the march past – which they did to loud cheers. The King reported that 'he was never at a review with which he was more delighted'.

That evening the King attended the Peers' Ball in the Assembly Rooms. The rooms had been transformed by Mr Murray. The doors opened at 8.00pm. There were huge traffic jams in George Street as carriages arrived to deposit those lucky enough to get invitations.

Those in Sedan chairs had an easier approach. The King arrived at 9.45pm. He was still wearing his uniform of the afternoon and riding boots. He sat on the prepared throne and watched enthralled as guests danced to Nathaniel Gow's music. After about two hours he left but the Ball continued until after 1.00am.

On Saturday 24 August, the Honours of Scotland were returned from the Palace to the Castle. The King meanwhile was resting at Dalkeith Palace. It was only on that morning that he confirmed to Scott that he would attend the dinner arranged for that evening in Parliament Hall and that he would attend the church service organised for St Giles' Kirk on the Sunday. The strain on Scott must have been immense.

The Dinner in Parliament Hall had three hundred invited guests. Again the venue had been transformed by William Murray, owner of the Theatre Royal. Great lustres in scarlet and gold were suspended from the hammer-beam ceiling. The largest cost £1,200 (equivalent to about £97,000 today). The guests gathered in the Signet Library at 4.30pm and were summoned to their places an hour later. The King arrived in his scarlet Field Marshal's uniform to be greeted by the Lord Provost and Baillies of the City. As guests worked their way through an enormous menu – at least fifteen courses were served – they were entertained by Nathaniel Gow's band and the band of the 77th Regiment. An incredible forty-seven toasts were proposed. The Royal Toast was followed by the National Anthem accompanied by fireworks in Parliament Square and artillery salutes. The King, much moved, replied:

> Words fail me were I to attempt to describe to you my feeling ... I consider this one of the proudest days of my life and you may judge with what truth and with what sincerity and with what delight I drink all your good healths.

Later he rose again to propose his own personal toast of thanks. Raising his glass George toasted: 'All the chieftains and all the clans of Scotland, and may God bless the Land of Cakes.' Exhausted the King left at 9.00pm long before the round of toasts was finished. However, before he returned to Dalkeith Place, he created the Lord Provost a baronet. Overwhelmed, Arbuthnot sank to his knees and kissed the King's hand.

The Assembly Rooms, George Street, from *Modern Athens Displayed* by Thomas Shepherd, 1829.

Next morning St Giles' Kirk opened at 7.00am. All ticket-holders had been instructed to be in their places by 9.00am. The King arrived at 11.15, accompanied by the Earl of Errol bearing the Sword of State, wearing again the uniform of a Field-Marshall with the green sash of the Order of the Thistle. George had come to Edinburgh accompanied by a posse of artists. Now he was watched by David Wilkie, J.M.W. Turner and William Collins, each of whom intended to paint the scene.

On Monday, the King made a private visit to Holyrood Palace. He spent fifty minutes in Mary, Queen of Scots' private apartments where David Rizzio had been murdered before the Queen in March 1566. At 9.30pm he returned to The Assembly Rooms in George Street this time for the Caledonian Hunt Ball. Once again it was an evening of tartan and Scottish country dancing with music by Nathaniel Gow. The King stood on a dais and shouted encouragement to the dancers. He left at 11.30 looking very tired. Clearly the pace was beginning to tell on the grossly overweight George who was also suffering severely from the effects of gout. So next day he absented himself from the laying of the foundation stone of the National Monument on Calton Hill. Instead the stone

The Theatre Royal on Princes Street, from *Modern Athens Displayed* by Thomas Shepherd, 1829.

was laid by the Duke of Hamilton, Scotland's Grand Master Mason.

After a small private supper party at Melville Castle, the King attended a performance of *Rob Roy* at the Theatre Royal. The theatre was packed. People had been waiting since 1.00pm to get a seat. The dragoons had to be called in to control the crowds. The King arrived at 8.00pm. The play chosen was performed at the King's request. The King was greeted with a roar and then the whole cast took to the stage to sing the National Anthem. George spent three hours at the theatre and enjoyed himself immensely. At his departure the National Anthem was sung again this time with a new verse written by Scott:

> Bright beams are soon o'ercast,
> Soon our brief hour is past,
>   Losing our King.
> Honoured, beloved, and dear.
> Still shall his parting ear
> Our latest accents hear,
>   God save the King.

King George at Hopetoun House.

The Commemorative Medal for George IV's visit.

George was again quite overcome and wept tears of joy.

The visit was now nearly at an end. On Wednesday George made a private visit to Newbattle Abbey where he was entertained by the Marquis of Lothian. That evening the King hosted a small dinner party at Dalkeith Palace. Twelve of Lord Breadalbane's Highlanders danced reels and Strathspeys for the King.

Friday 23 August was to be George's last day in Scotland. He travelled by coach from Dalkeith Palace to Hopetoun House where he was welcomed by the 4th Earl of Hopetoun. Once again huge crowds had gathered in the rain to welcome the King. The Earl greeted the King in his new uniform as Captain-General of the Royal Company of Archers, made at a cost of £400. The King ate a small lunch washed down by three glasses of wine; admired the ten children of the Earl and Countess and borrowed a sword to knight Adam Ferguson, Keeper of the Regalia and the artist Henry Raeburn. The King then was driven to Port Hopetoun where he embarked on the *Royal George*.

The visit was over. It had been an outstanding success and the King was truly grateful. The Home Secretary Robert Peel wrote to the Lord Provost: 'He takes leave of Scotland with the most cordial feelings of affection toward her people, and with the deepest anxiety to promote their welfare.'

A special medal was struck celebrating the visit and as a 'thank you', George agreed to a request from Walter Scott for the return of Mons Meg, the iconic medieval cannon that had been removed from Edinburgh Castle in 1754. In return, Edinburgh named the new access route from the High Street to the south, George IV Bridge in the King's honour. Finally in 1831, a very flattering statue of the King by Francis Chantrey (who was then knighted), was unveiled in Edinburgh's George Street.

OVERLEAF. The statue of George IV in George Street, Edinburgh.

CHAPTER 17

The Great Fire
of 1824

Two years after the visit of King George IV, John Kay would almost certainly have been an eyewitness to the disastrous fire that at one time threatened to destroy the whole of the Old Town of Edinburgh. After a series of damaging fires, the Council had decided to form their own fire brigade. The previous practice had been to rely on neighbours, the burgh's chimney sweeps (the Tron Men) or local volunteers to tackle blazes. The Old Town of Edinburgh was particularly at risk given the narrowness of the closes and the height of so many of the tenement buildings. There was also the fact that most buildings depended on open coal fires for their heating and cooking. Many could not afford closed lanterns so relied on unguarded candles for their lighting.

In 1824, Edinburgh Council created the UK's first municipal Fire Brigade and took the brave decision to appoint a young twenty-four years' old builder, James Braidwood, as the burgh's first Firemaster. Braidwood had been born in Edinburgh and educated at the High School. He had joined his father's building firm and had trained as a surveyor. He thus had a very good working knowledge of building construction. At his interview he had impressed with his forward-thinking ideas as to how the planned fire brigade should operate. Braidwood recruited his first firemen, known as 'pioneers' from men familiar with the building trade – masons, plumbers and carpenters. Realising that the height of Edinburgh's tenements would prove a particular challenge, he also recruited former sailors who were used to climbing at heights and to handling heavy equipment. Braidwood put great emphasis on training and physical fitness for himself and his men.

Within just two months of the brigade's formation, they were called into action. The fire started at 10.00pm on the night of 15 November 1824 in the premises of an engraver on the second floor of a tenement in Old Assembly Close, on the south side of the High Street – straight across the road from John Kay's home. The fire quickly engulfed the offices of the *Edinburgh Evening Courant*. Undeterred the paper's staff moved across the High Street to temporary premises and continued to publish.

The burgh's Fire Brigade was quickly on the scene but their work was hampered by the height of the tenement buildings and the narrowness of the close which prevented the fire engines from getting near to the blaze. They also struggled to find a source of water. The flames spread rapidly, blown by a strong south-west breeze. Soon the entire tenement was a mass of flame.

The fire spread quickly. A strong wind blew sparks and burning embers into the air and soon dozens of properties were alight. Huge crowds gathered to witness the destruction. Building after building caught fire. The Fire Brigade could do nothing to stop the spread of the flames. James Grant gives a vivid eyewitness account in his *Old and New Edinburgh:*

> While these tall and stately edifices were yielding to destruc-
> tion, the night grew calm and still, and the sparks emitted
> by the flames shot upwards as if spouted from a volcano, and
> descended like the thickest drift or snow-storm, affecting the
> respiration of all. A dusky, lurid red tinged the clouds, and
> the glare shone on the Castle walls, the rocks of the Calton
> [Hill] the beetling crags [Arthur's Seat], and all the city
> spires. Scores of lofty chimneys, set on fire by the falling
> sparks, added to the growing horror of the scene; and for a
> considerable time the Tron Church was completely
> enveloped in this perilous shower of embers.

All that night and the next day the fire spread. To the choking smoke and fiery embers was now added the thick masonry dust as some of the burnt tenement buildings came crashing down. Then at 9.00am on the morning of 16 November, the fire reached the Tron

The Great Fire in the High Street, 16 November 1824: the steeple of the Tron Kirk
is in flames (W. Turner DeLond, 1825).

Kirk. As word spread, bewigged lawyers ran out from the nearby
Court House in Parliament Close. Amongst them was Henry
Cockburn, later to be Lord Cockburn the well-known judge and
author. This is how he described the scene in his famous *Memorials
of His Time.*

> These fires broke out on the evening of Monday the 15th of
> November 1824, on the south side of the High Street about
> half-way between the Tron Church and St Giles' Cathedral;
> and before morning a range of houses six or seven stories
> high, with fifteen windows in front, and extending back
> almost to the Cowgate – as dense a mass of buildings as was
> perhaps in the world, was a burnt shell. People thought this
> bad enough . . . But about noon the next day an alarm was
> given that the Tron Church was on fire. We ran out from the
> Court, gowned and wigged. And saw that it was the steeple
> . . . Some of the sparks of the preceding night had nestled in
> it, and had at last blown its dry bones into flame. There could
> not have been a more beautiful firework . . . It was one
> hour's brilliant blaze. The spire was too high and too

combustionable to admit of any attempt to save it. So that we had nothing to do but admire. And it certainly was beautiful. The conflagration was long presided over by a calm and triumphant gilded cock on the top of the spire, which seemed to look on the people and to listen to the crackling with disdain. But it was undermined at last, and dived down into the burning gulph, followed by the upper half of the steeple.

The Tron Kirk lay to the east of the main blaze and it was hoped that the fires would now burn themselves out. But to the dismay of the hundreds of onlookers, many of whom had travelled up from their New Town residences to see the scene for themselves, the fires now spread westward towards St Giles' Kirk and Parliament Close. Rumours now spread that this could only be the work of arsonists intent on torching the whole of the Old Town. *The Edinburgh Evening Courant* (operating from temporary accommodation on the north side of the High Street) reported that:

> About 5 o'clock [on the morning of 16 November] the fire had proceeded so far downwards in the building occupied by the *Courant* office, that the upper part of the front fell inwards with a dreadful crash, the concussion driving the flames into the middle of the street . . . By 9 o'clock the steeple of the Tron Church was discovered to be on fire; the pyramid became a mass of flame, the lead of the roof poured over the masonry in molten streams and fell with a crash . . . But the church was saved chiefly by a powerful engine belonging to the Board of Ordnance.
>
> The fire was now stopped, but the horror and dismay of the people increased when at ten that night, a new one broke forth in the devoted Parliament Close [lying to the south of St Giles] in the attic of a tenement eleven stories in height overlooking the Cowgate. As this house was far to the windward of the other fire, it was quite impossible that one could have caused another – a conclusion which forced itself upon the minds of all, together with the startling belief that

OPPOSITE. The Great Fire in Parliament Square (W. Turner DeLond, 1825).

Looking west up the High Street towards St Giles' Kirk. John Kay's house
is on the right (W. Turner DeLond, 1825).

some desperate incendiaries had resolved to destroy the city:
while many went about exclaiming that it was a special
punishment sent from Heaven upon the people for their
sins.

Whether it was indeed the work of arsonists or divine retribution
for the sins of the city was a matter for another day. Now the task
was to preserve the historic Old Town. People threw themselves into
the task of saving St Giles and the buildings of Parliament Close.
Several leading members of the legal profession distinguished
themselves including the Lord Advocate, Sir William Rae. With his
jacket off and his sleeves rolled up he helped pump water for one
of the fire engines. As the sweat poured down his smoke-blackened
face, one of the Lord Advocate's fellow-helpers, reportedly slapped
him on the back and congratulated him 'Weel done, my lord!' Rich
and poor lined up to pass buckets of water drawn from the town
wells.

This dramatic scene in Parliament Close shows the panic and
confusion caused by the fire. Mounted soldiers try to maintain
order amongst the terrified people. John Kay and his wife could

well have been in that crowd trying to salvage items from his workshop. The equestrian statue of Charles II has been taken down to preserve it from melting in the heat. The flames on the right are engulfing John Kay's workshop which was totally destroyed. The reporter of the *Courant* vividly described the struggle:

> The scene was now awfully grand ... The whole horizon was completely enveloped in lurid flame ... Spectacular columns of flame shot up majestically into the atmosphere, which assumed a lurid, dusky, reddish hue; dismay, daring, suspense, fear, sat upon different countenances, intensely expressive of their various emotions; the bronzed faces of the firemen shone momentarily from under their caps as their heads were raised at each successive stroke of the engines; and the very element by which they attempted to extinguish the conflagration seemed itself a stream of liquid fire. The County Hall [The City Chambers, formerly the Royal Exchange] at one time appeared like a palace of light and the venerable steeple of St Giles reared itself amid the bright flames like a spectre awakened to behold the fall and ruin of the devoted City.

St Giles and Parliament Hall were saved. It was Edinburgh's weather that finally came to the rescue. Fortunately the wind eased and a downpour on 17 November eventually put out the fires. Thirteen lives were lost including those of two firemen and many people were injured. The damage was immense with twenty-five tenements, some eleven storeys high, totally destroyed and many others damaged. Amongst the buildings burnt down in Parliament Close itself was the workshop of John Kay. This almost certainly accounts for the loss of a considerable number of the plates engraved by Kay. The stretch of the High Street running from Parliament Close down to the Tron Kirk had suffered severe damage. Behind these houses, the closes and wynds running down to the Cowgate were a devastation of collapsed buildings and smoking ruins. The spire of the Tron Kirk had fallen but fortunately the church itself was saved. An estimated four hundred to five hundred families were left homeless.

Several of the burnt-out tenements were dangerous and threatened imminent collapse. Lacking any sort of suitable equipment,

the Town Council was at a loss as to what to do. One suggestion was to bring cannon from the Castle and to blast the ruins down. Help came from an unexpected source. Captain Hope, the commanding officer of HMS *Brisk* which was at that time anchored at Leith, volunteered the services of some of his crew. A squad of forty sailors duly appeared and after two days struggle they managed, with the help of iron cables, ropes and chains to pull down the worst of the ruined buildings.

And what of James Braidwood? There was some initial criticism with councillors complaining that it had taken too long for the firemen to get into action and that they had been unable to get the fires under quick control. Braidwood though strongly defended his actions and the actions of his men. He pointed out that their work had been hampered by councillors giving orders and counter-orders to him and to his men. The public backed Braidwood. He was now widely praised for his efforts. The Council was forced to agree that in any future fire, it was the Firemaster who was in charge, not individual councillors. Braidwood was 'head-hunted'. He was appointed as the first Firemaster of London in 1833 and, at the age of 61, was tragically killed while on duty in 1861 at the Tooley Street Dock Fire.

OPPOSITE. The statue of James Braidwood erected in 2008 in Parliament Square.

CHAPTER 18

'The Celebrated Caricaturist, Engraver, Print Seller, and Picture Dealer ...'

When Hugh Paton published *Kay's Portraits* in 1837, he identified this portrait of Archibald Campbell, one of the City Officers, as the last portrait drawn and etched by John Kay 'then about eighty years of age'. Like many of his fellow citizens at that time, Campbell was a Highlander. It was claimed that when his mother died in Edinburgh, Campbell arranged for her coffin to be taken back to the Highlands to be buried beside her relations. It was widely rumoured that the hearse returned to Edinburgh filled with illicit whisky for Campbell. When he was challenged by a friend on the subject, Kay records Campbell as having replied: 'Wow, man there's nae harm done. I only carried awa' the body, and brought back the speerit.'

The last dated portrait seems to be that of James Mackoull (page 230), alias Captain Moffat, which is inscribed '1821'. Mackoull was a notorious pick-pocket, thief and bank robber who was born in London in 1763. His mother was a well-known thief, and one of his brothers was hanged for theft.

Mackoull fled justice in London and, after a spell on the Continent calling himself Captain Moffat, he arrived in Edinburgh in 1805 and continued his career as a pickpocket and thief. Mackoull was staying in nearby New Street when Thomas Begbie, a messenger for the British Linen Bank, was murdered and robbed of £4,000 in

OPPOSITE. Archibald Campbell, City Officer.

Tweeddale Court on the evening of 13 November 1806. The murderer was never caught. Mackoull fled Edinburgh but returned in 1811 and was part of a gang who robbed the Paisley Union Bank in Queen Street of £20,000. Again Mackoull managed to escape justice. He was eventually arrested on his return to Edinburgh and convicted in 1820. He was locked up in the new Calton Gaol awaiting sentence for his crimes. He was then questioned about the murder of Begbie as the authorities had at last been able to place Mackoull near the scene of the crime. (Mackoull had given an alibi that he had been in Dublin in November 1806. This was now known to be false.) Mackoull denied his guilt but suffered a seizure and died in prison on 22 December 1821. It is quite remarkable that Kay could still produce such detailed and accurate portraits at such an advanced age. (He was then seventy-nine years of age.)

His friend and future publisher Hugh Paton has left us this charming description of Kay in his later years:

> In his outward appearance, he was a slender, straight old man, of middle size, and usually dressed in a garb of antique cut, of simple habits and quiet, unassuming manners.

John Kay died in his High Street home in March 1826. The *Edinburgh Evening Courant* carried this short death notice:

> Death Notice
> Died on the 25th ultimo at his house, no. 227 High Street, Mr John Kay, in the eighty-fourth year of his age.
> (*Edinburgh Evening Courant,* Saturday 25 March 1826)

John Kay's death marked the end of an era. For nearly forty years, this talented artist had faithfully recorded so much of the vibrant Edinburgh scene. Clearly there must still have been a demand for his engraved portraits. His widow, Margaret Scott, was determined to carry on with the business as best she could. This advert placed in the *Courant* would suggest that Mrs Kay had been helping her late husband in the production of his engraved plates.

For whatever reason, Margaret Kay left the High Street home

OPPOSITE. James Mackoull on trial in Edinburgh.

MRS KAY begs respectfully to intimate to her Friends and the Public, that since the death of her husband, the late Mr JOHN KAY, Picture Dealer, she continues to carry on the business on her own ac· count, and has now on sale a good collection of PIC- TURES, OLD ENGRAVINGS, and ETCHINGS ; also of the well-known CURIOUS PORTRAITS etched by her late Husband, complete sets of which she is now preparing, and will have ready for delivery in a short time.

227, High Street, Edinburgh,
20th May, 1826.

Mrs Kay's advert in the *Edinburgh Evening Courant*, May 1826.

that she had shared with John Kay. The *Edinburgh Street Directory* for 1833–4 records that 'Mrs Margaret Scott (Kay) Picture Dealer' was living in 76 Nicholson Street just south of the Old Town. In 1835–6, Margaret Scott is living at 2 Drummond Street, close to Nicholson Street. She is again recorded as a 'Picture Dealer'.

There is no way of knowing whether the business proved to be a success or whether the changes of address meant that Margaret Kay was struggling. However, clearly there was still an interest and a market for Kay's work. The *Courant* reported that 'Mrs Margaret Kay (nee Scott) had died 25th November 1835.' Her executors proceeded to organise a sale of John Kay's effects which he had left to Margaret.

It should be noted that the advert refers specifically to '356 plates'. As stated previously we will never know how many plates had been purchased by offended subjects and then destroyed; how many were lost in the Great Fire or how many were (and still are?) in private hands. John Kay had always intended to publish a collected edition of his portraits. Whether it was lack of time or funding, the task was never completed in his lifetime. What is clear from the advert, however, is that he had started to write biographical notes (the 'Descriptive Catalogue, full of amusing anecdotes realtive to the subjects of the plates'). Again we have no way of knowing just how many of the published portraits were covered by Kay's notes.

The published sale catalogue would suggest that as well as selling

11, Hanover Street, Feb. 15.

SALE OF THE WORKS AND OTHER GENUINE PROPERTY OF

The late Mr JOHN KAY, of Edinburgh, the celebrated Caricaturist, Engraver, Print-seller, and Picture Dealer.

IN consequence of the decease of Mrs KAY, widow of the above celebrated Artist, the whole of his Works and other Property have passed into the hands of Executors, who have instructed Mr WALKER of the AGENCY OFFICE to sell the same in his rooms, opposite the College, by PUBLIC AUCTION, on Monday the 22d day of February 1836, and following days. Sale to commence at twelve o'clock.

Mr WALKER begs to call the attention of all interested in such property, and the public generally, to this important sale. The property consists of—

1. 356 Plates, being the works of Kay. Along with the Chest of Plates will be sold a curious holograph Descriptive Catalogue, full of amusing anecdotes, relative to the subjects of the Plates. These Plates, if got up in sets along with the Catalogue, will be one of the most unique and interesting productions ever presented to the lovers of taste, story, and amusement, and must be a valuable investment of capital to a spirited publisher.

N.B.—Mr Walker warrants that not a single impression has been taken from these Plates since Mrs Kay's death.

The advert placed in the *Edinburgh Evening Courant*, February 1836.

prints of his engravings, Kay was also a substantial art dealer. In addition to the surviving plates, nine sets of Kay's prints and twenty-three individual prints, the catalogue lists no less than seven hundred and nineteen other prints and engravings for sale. The catalogue also included eighteen 'very fine minatures on Ivory, by Kay when young. Neither he nor his widow would part with them during their lives'.

One man who was determined to purchase the plates was Hugh Paton, a woodcarver, who was an old friend of John Kay. Paton had

CATALOGUE

OF THE WORKS AND OTHER GENUINE PROPERTY

OF THE

LATE MR JOHN KAY OF EDINBURGH,

The Celebrated Caricaturist Engraver, Print Seller, and Picture Dealer, to be SOLD by Mr WALKER of the AGENCY OFFICE, in his Rooms, opposite the College, on MONDAY the 22d day of February 1836, and following Days.

SALE TO COMMENCE AT TWELVE O'CLOCK.

FRAMED PRINTS, &c.

1 Landscape, Water Colours, varnished.
2 Harbour and Shipping.   do.
3 Man shading his face from Torch.
4 Full length Engraving by Jones of Prince of Wales, by Reynolds,
5 Kissing the Hem of his Garment, water colour, varnished.
6 View of Frivoli, engraved from Gasper Poussin's Painting.
           1st Lot, 25 Engravings.
           2d Lot, 25   do.
7 The Evening, engraved by Vivares, from Vernet's Painting.
8 Hon. Thomas Erskine, engraved by Sharp
9 John Harrison, Esq. of Leeds.
10 2 Prints by William Hone, London.
11 Card Playing.
12 Le Bourguemestre Syae Ami, de Rembrant.
13 Playing Cards, W. O. Arkersfoot, 1626, engraved by Molyn.
14 Prince William Henry.
15 King of Prussia,   } One Lot.
   Queen of Do.   }
16 Billiards.
17 Watered Coloured Landscape and Queen Anne, 1 lot.
           3d Lot, 25 Engravings.
           4th Lot, 25   do.
           5th Lot, 25   do.
18 Thomas Paine, Author of the Rights of Man, &c.
19 Coat-of-Arms. Surgeon-Barbers
20 Raised Gilded Head.
21 Curious Coloured and Raised Bird.

been persuaded to buy the plates by Robert Maidment, the City Advocate, who appreciated the importance of Kay's work. Maidment provided the text for the first portraits assembled by Paton but pressure of work saw the task being passed to a young journalist, James Paterson, a native of Ayrshire, newly returned from Dublin. His brother William was an apprentice with Hugh Paton. Paterson was given a 'trial' by Paton and asked to write an entry for Vincenzo Lunardi, the balloonist. This was well-received by Hugh Paton ('This is a good article') and Paterson was hired for a salary of 15/- (75p) a week. In his *Autobiographical Reminiscences* published in 1871, Paterson claimed that: 'From thence the whole labour of writing the sketches and tracing out information devolved upon me.'

Paterson certainly threw himself into his task. He researched the characters and where possible he met with surviving subjects and the families of those who had died to gather information for his entries. Paton prepared letters of introduction for Paterson to help him with this exercise. Much information was gained from Andrew Smellie, the son of the well-known printer and publisher, William Smellie. Paterson researched at the Advocates' Library at Parliament Hall where he scanned back numbers of contemporary newspapers such as the *Caledonian Mercury,* the *Edinburgh Evening Courant* and the *Scots' Magazine.* He was helped by Mr Haig, the under-librarian. Paterson was also allowed access to Maidment's personal library.

The two volumes, containing 329 plates, took three years to produce. In anticipation of publication, Hugh Paton advertised for subscribers to pre-order copies. The response was very encouraging. In total 572 copies were ordered by subscribers whose names were printed in the first edition of *Kay's Portraits* which was published in 1837. The first name entered was that of the young Queen Victoria who had only just ascended the throne. She was followed by her mother, the Duchess of Kent. Amongst the other subscribers were the Duke of Buccleuch, the Earl of Dalhousie, the Earl of Lauderdale, the Duke of Marlborough and Viscount Melville. Of the subscribers, sixty-six per cent were Edinburgh citizens, including Lord Cockburn, Lord Jeffrey, Professor James Syme, Surgeon to the Queen, Sir John Stewart Forbes of Pitsligo whose grandfather had been drawn by Kay, and Dr Robert Knox the

OPPOSITE. The first page of the sale catalogue.

OF

ORIGINAL PORTRAITS

AND

CARICATURE ETCHINGS,

BY THE LATE

JOHN KAY,

MINIATURE PAINTER, EDINBURGH;

WITH

BIOGRAPHICAL SKETCHES AND ILLUSTRATIVE ANECDOTES.

VOL. I.

NISI DOMINUS FRUSTRA

EDINBURGH:

HUGH PATON, CARVER AND GILDER

To Her Majesty Queen Victoria,

AND HER ROYAL HIGHNESS THE DUCHESS OF KENT.

MDCCCXXXVII.

anatomist who had recently purchased bodies from the infamous Burke and Hare.

Another interesting subscriber was James Burnes, Provost of Montrose and a cousin of the poet Robert Burns. One of his sons was Sir Alexander Burnes. Sir Alexander was appointed as Political Resident at Kabul in September 1839. Afghanistan was a country in turmoil. At the very outset of the insurrection which took place in favour of Dost Mohammed, on 2 November 1841, the thirty-six-year-old Colonel Burnes was slaughtered, along with his brother Charles, and seven other officers. This outrage was to lead to an invasion by a British force which was then totally destroyed as it retreated from Kabul in 1842. Some 16,000 lives were lost. The only British survivor was the Scottish medical officer Dr William Brydon. Brydon's life was saved by a copy of the Edinburgh-published *Blackwood's Magazine* sent to him by his mother. He had put it under his hat to protect his head from the extreme cold. The magazine took the force of a sword blow that would have certainly killed Brydon.

There were 399 copies ordered by booksellers. These included Mr E. Chainley of Newcastle (two copies), William & Robert Chambers of Edinburgh (three copies) George Gallie, of Glasgow (twenty-nine copies) and Messrs Smith, Elder & Co of London (one hundred and thirteen copies). There seems to have been a very high level of interest amongst the public as Hugh Paton felt it necessary to publish an apology to any whose names had been omitted:

> Though very desirous to have the List of Subscribers as complete as possible, it has been found impracticable to give the names of all those who have honoured this Work with their patronage. Many copies have been supplied through the medium of booksellers, considerable difficulty has been experienced in obtaining returns from those for whom they had orders. As an instance, it may be mentioned that one house, taking upwards of one hundred copies, has not yet furnished the name of a single Subscriber.

OPPOSITE. Title page of the first edition of *Kay's Portraits* published in 1837.

The publication of *Kay's Portraits* was a resounding success. There were several very favourable reviews:

> Kay lived at a fortunate period ... All classes of society were then in a manner close packed in the Old Town, not diffused through the wide expanse of the New ... Edinburgh was one great carnival from one end of the year to the other, and almost all the characters were supported with the unction of genius. This strange masquerade has been immortalised in three hundred and fifty-six engravings by the kindred genius of Kay.
>
> *(London Literary Gazette)*

> We think it a work deserving of every praise and encouragement, and which is honourable equally to the talents of Kay, and to the enterprise of Mr. Paton the spirited publisher.
>
> *(Weekly Chronicle)*

> There is no one, indeed, to whom the quaint style of the portraits, and the familiar chit-chat of the letter press, will not be both amusing and interesting; and we cordially commend the work to our readers.
>
> *(The Scotsman)*

> The work is really one of which Edinburgh ought to be proud ... Kay's portraits have always maintained a high reputation in Edinburgh, as faithful and genuine resemblances of the eccentric or distinguished men, on whom he exercised his native and self-taught talent.
>
> *(Edinburgh Evening Courant)*

This success saw a second edition being published by Paton in 1842. The plates were then purchased by the London publishers Adam and Charles Black who produced a third edition costing 8 guineas (£8.40) in 1877. Tragically the publishers then destroyed John Kay's surviving plates to prevent a further original edition being published. Kay's beautiful engraved plates were dumped in a flooded quarry.

The Museum of Edinburgh, situated near the foot of the city's historic Royal Mile, has a remarkable tribute to John Kay. In 1844 a group of well-known Scottish artists including Sir David Wilkie and David Roberts collaborated in producing a painting of Parliament Close in Edinburgh as it was before the Great Fire of 1824. The view depicted is looking northwards towards St Giles' Kirk as it would have looked from the window of John Kay's workshop (see Plate 13). The painting is very much an acknowledgement of the genius of John Kay as the Close is filled with characters from *Kay's Portraits*. Standing in the foreground to the right of the statue of Charles II are William Smellie and Andrew Bell with his distinctive large nose and knock-knees.

John Kay was an undoubted celebrity in his own lifetime. Writing in 1835 just nine years after Kay's death, Robert Chambers had this to say about John Kay in his *Biographical Dictionary of Eminent Scotsmen*:

> To speak of his portraits as caricatures is doing them signal injustice. They were the most exact and faithful likenesses that could have been reproduced by any mode of art. He drew the man as he walked the street every day; his gait, his costume, every peculiarity of his appearance, done to a point, and no defect perceptible except the stiffness of the figures.

John Kay had a remarkable eye for detail; a skill still obvious in his final portraits drawn when he was approaching eighty. He seemed to have the ability to catch an expression or a physical characteristic. If William Creech is to be believed (see page 76) then he was able to achieve this with not much more than a single glance. There are some portraits where Kay has clearly spent more time in achieving an astonishing attention to detail. The portrait of Angelo Tremamondo is a good example. Here Kay has shown his subject on horseback set against delicately drawn trees. Tremamondo had spent time in London as the Royal Fencing Master to the sons of George III. He gained something of a reputation as a duellist so chose to move northwards to Edinburgh where he established himself as a riding master. Tremamondo died in 1802 at the advanced age of 86.

The portrait of William Wilson, 'Mortar Willie', is one of Kay's finest portraits. It was drawn in 1815, just before Willie's death, when he

John Kay's portrait of Angelo Tremamondo.

was in his 107th year. Almost certainly this is a posed portrait where Kay has visited Willie in the apothecary's shop of Mr Burt in the Lawnmarket where he worked for many years. Having worked in his native Perthshire as an agricultural labourer, Willie joined the British Army and fought against Bonnie Prince Charlie at Culloden. In this portrait Kay has displayed close attention to the detail of Willie's clothing. Unusually Kay has highlighted the effects of the light coming in at the window. There is no humour here nor any attempt to make fun of the character drawn. This is one of Kay's

John Kay's portrait of William Wilson, 'Mortar Willie'.

most sympathetic portraits and you feel that this is indeed, in the words of Robert Chambers, 'an exact and faithful likeness'.

Kay's caricaturist contemporaries, Isaac Cruikshank (a fellow Scot), his son George Cruikshank and James Gilray, were notorious for their often cruel social and political satire. By contrast, Kay, while he was not afraid to express his opinions as in the case of Thomas Muir, drew his portraits with a delicate personal touch and often graced them with a gentle humour. As we saw with Deacon Brodie, Kay would often include a relevant topical allusion that added to

The Commemorative Stone to John Kay in Greyfriars Kirkyard, Edinburgh.

the story that he was endeavouring to tell about his subject. He was not afraid to draw his characters as he saw them physically and it seems that the subjects of these portraits rarely took offence. Kay was justifiably much-admired and much-loved by his contemporaries.

John Kay's legacy is a unique glimpse of life in Edinburgh during one of the most fascinating periods in the history of the city. We are very much in John Kay's debt.

Bibliography

Further Reading

Armstrong, Murray, *The Liberty Tree: The Stirring Story of Thomas Muir And Scotland's First Fight For Democracy* (Word Power, 2014)
Brodie, Alexander, *The Scottish Enlightenment Reader* (Canongate, 1999)
Birrell, J. F., *An Edinburgh Alphabet* (Merat Press, 1980)
Buchan, James, *Capital of the Mind: How Edinburgh Changed the World* (Birlinn, 2007)
Catford, F. E., *Edinburgh: The Story of a City* (Hutchinson, 1975)
Coghill, Hamish, *Lost Edinburgh* (Birlinn, 2008)
Cosh, Mary, *Edinburgh: the Golden Age* (Birlinn, 2014)
Dick, David, *Who was Who in the Royal Mile Edinburgh* (Clerkington, 1997)
Evans, Hilary and Mary, *John Kay of Edinburgh: Barber, Miniaturist and Social Commentator, 1742–1826* (1973)
Fry, Michael, *Edinburgh: A History of the City* (Pan, 2010)
Gibson, John S., *Deacon Brodie* (Saltire Society, 1992)
Grant, James, *Cassell's Old and New Edinburgh*, 3 vols (Nabu Press, 2010)
Harris, Stuart, *The Place Names of Edinburgh: Their Origins and History* (Steve Savage, 2010)
Massie, Alan, *Edinburgh* (Sinclair-Stevenson, 1994)
Melvin, Eric, *A Walk Down Edinburgh's Royal Mile* (CreateSpace, 2014)
Melvin, Eric, *A Walk through Edinburgh's New Town*(CreateSpace, 2014)
Morris, Albert, *Kay's Capital Characters* (Pentland Associates, 1996)
Prebble, John, *The King's Jaunt: King George IV in Scotland, 1822* (HarperCollins, 1988)
Ritchie, W. K., *Edinburgh in its Golden Age* (Longman, 1967)
Szatkowski, Sheila, *Capital Caricatures* (Birlinn, 2007)
Wilson, Daniel, *Memorials of Edinburgh: In the Olden Time* (Forgotten Books, 2016)
Youngson, A. J., *The Making of Classical Edinburgh* (Edinburgh University Press, 1966)

Primary Sources

Anonymous, *Information for His Majesty's Advocate, for His Highness's Interest against John Porteous 1736* (Gale, 2012)
Anonymous, *Proposals for Carrying on Certain Works in the City of Edinburgh* (1752)
Anonymous, *The Trial of Alexander Stewart, late Lord Provost of Edinburgh*, 1747
Arnot, Hugo, *The History of Edinburgh . . .*, 2nd edn (William Creech, 1788)

Bruce, James, *Travels to Discover the Source of the Nile*, 2nd edn (Archibald Constable, 1804)

Carlyle, Alexander, *Autobiography* (1860)

Chambers, Robert, *Traditions of Edinburgh*, 5th edn (Chambers, 1996)

Cockburn, Lord Henry, *Memorials of his Time* (Adam and Charles Black, 1856)

Creech, William, *An Account of the Trial of William Brodie and George Smith* (William Creech, 1788)

Creech, William, *Letters to Sir John Sinclair* (1793)

Edinburgh & Leith Post Office Directory

Edinburgh Evening Courant

Macaulay, Margaret, articles, *The Scottish Book Collector,* Vol. 5 no. 12; Vol. 6, No. 1 (1998)

Paton, Hugh, *Kay's Portraits*, 2 vols (Paton, 1837)

Robinson, George, 'Kay's Caricatures', *Scots Magazine,* February 1997

Roughead, William, *The Trial of Deacon Brodie* (Forgotten Books, 2012)

Tytler, James, *The Directory of Ladies of Pleasure in Edinburgh* (1779)

Some of these titles are out of print. A good source for locating such titles is: www.abebooks.co.uk

The City of Edinburgh Council Libraries have an excellent site of illustrated material relating to Edinburgh at www.capitalcollections.com

Picture Credits

The author is grateful to the following for permission to reproduce images:

Chiaroscuro Video Productions and Digital Arts (Peter Ross): pp. 6, 13, 29, 34, 50, 78, 80, 83, 84, 89, 91, 94, 98, 100, 103, 106, 108, 110, 112, 114, 115, 116, 118, 122, 123, 124, 125, 126, 127, 129, 131, 138, 139 (both), 141, 142, 145, 149, 150, 159, 165, 170, 174, 177, 187, 196, 229, 230

With the permission of the City of Edinburgh Council Museums and Galleries: Colour Plate 13

With the kind permission of the Edinburgh City Libraries – Edinburgh Room: pp. 9, 14, 16, 23, 27, 33, 42, 51, 63, 70–71, 101, 175, 20, 212, 221, 223, 224; Colour Plates 3, 9, 10, 12.

Eric Melvin – pp. i, vi, viii, 1, 5, 8, 17, 24, 36, 37, 43, 45, 47, 52, 54, 59, 60, 67, 69, 72, 73, 86, 92, 104, 119, 137, 143, 144, 147, 148, 154, 161, 164, 171, 180, 181, 182, 183, 185, 191, 193, 199, 203, 216 (both), 218, 226, 236, 240, 241, 242; Colour Plates 2, 5 and 11.

Reproduced by permission of the National Library of Scotland: pp. 163, 173, 195, 232, 233, 234

Reproduced by permission of the National Library of Scotland Maps: pp. 64–65, 74.

Reproduced by permission of the Scottish National Portrait Gallery: pp. 201('The Honours of Scotland'. The discovery of the Scottish Regalia, Sir David Wilkie), 210 (George IV – 'The First laird in Aw Scotia', artist unknown); Colour Plates 1 (Self-portrait, John Kay), 4 (Prince Charles Edward Stuart, 1720–1788. Eldest Son of Prince James Francis Edward Stuart, Allan Ramsay), 6 (David Hume, 1711–1776. Historian and philosopher, Allan Ramsay, Bequeathed by Mrs Macdonald Hume to the National Gallery of Scotland and transferred), 7 (George Drummond, 1687–1766. Lord Provost of Edinburgh, Sir George Chalmers), 8 (James Craig, 1739–1795. Architect, David Allan).

Scottish Pictures (Ian Smith): pp. 130, 214, 215.

Index

Page references in **bold** indicate pages featuring portraits by John Kay.